OPEN MANAGEMENT

OPEN MANAGEMENT

Guides to Successful Practice

PAUL W. CUMMINGS

 A DIVISION OF AMERICAN MANAGEMENT ASSOCIATIONS

Library of Congress Cataloging in Publication Data

Cummings, Paul W
    Open management.

    Includes index.
    1. Management.   I. Title.
HD31.C83   658   79-54832
ISBN 0-8144-5522-0

© 1980 AMACOM
A division of American Management Associations, New York.

First Printing

*This book is dedicated to
my mother, my wife, my daughter, and my son—
whose patience, enthusiasm, and encouragement
far outlasted mine.*

PREFACE

This book presents a series of practical and successful solutions to "people problems"—solutions that are applicable to all levels of management in the public and private sectors of industry and business. *Open Management* encourages participative management and democratic leadership styles by concentrating on the worth, value, and dignity of the individual employee in our contemporary work world. The book presents and develops various techniques and alternative courses of action to readers to help them grow and become more effective managers.

Specifically, the format for each of the 12 chapters is built around the identification of several major people problems all managers face today. Several techniques for solving these problems are offered and checklists are presented as an aid to reviewing and reinforcing the material learned in each chapter.

PAUL W. CUMMINGS

ACKNOWLEDGMENTS

Over the past 30 years, many individuals have had an important influence on my management development and thinking, which has resulted in much of the subject matter contained in this book. To all of them, I extend my deep gratitude.

I would be remiss, however, if I did not specifically acknowledge my present employer, Heckett, a Division of Harsco, Inc., and my immediate supervisor, R. J. Shingleton, Vice President of Industrial Relations and Personnel. I want also to thank Ms. Jackie Hughes, a high school English teacher in the Mount Lebanon School District of Pittsburgh, Pennsylvania, who more than ably assisted me in overcoming many grammatical obstacles.

Finally, I thank my wife, Shirley, for her help in typing and retyping the manuscript, but most especially for sharing and bearing the many frustrations and disappointments we have encountered on our venturesome excursion through life.

CONTENTS

1 AUTHORITY

The Mainspring of Management

Defining managerial authority is like trying to hit a moving target. The only difference is that you can usually see a target, whereas authority cannot be perceived until it is exercised by the person who possesses it.

Authority is usually exercised in work organizations either by written word (letters, memos, directives, and policies) or by oral communication. In some cases, however, oral or written communications are not needed as a demonstration of authority. If the president of a company walks into the conference room in the middle of a training program for middle managers and sits down to observe the session, suddenly the participants seem to sit up a little straighter and to show a higher degree of attention and interest.

Industrial sociologists view authority in the work organization as a special form of power. Power is usually considered to be the ability of individuals to have their will obeyed. Hence, authority is a function of a legitimate position in a defined hierarchy. Effective authorities in

1

our society, however, recognize that they exercise their power *only because others are willing to accept it as such.*

The basis for authority

In our industrial democracy authority is primarily based on law. We elect legislative representatives at the local, county, state, and federal levels to represent us and make laws to protect us. In so doing we delegate our authority to these representatives. When an individual goes into business, he or she must adhere to the laws that have been established concerning that business. The authority to own a business and all the things that comprise that business (buildings, machinery, tools, offices) and to administer their use for a profit is further supported and upheld by laws. Therefore, law essentially works for and is acceptable to most of us because we are willing to exchange some small degree of our personal freedom for the security of living in a lawful community and working in a lawful enterprise.

Another basis of authority is ownership. Owning a business gives the owner the authority to contract for individuals' skills and services, to assign authority. Thus, a manager's authority is derived from holding a job within the business organization. For instance, in a public corporation the stockholders own the company and transmit their collective authority to the board of directors. The directors transmit their authority to the president, who in turn distributes authority throughout the organization to various levels of individuals called managers. Therefore, your authority as a manager has been assigned to you by the owners of the organization, who are protected by the law.

Real authority, however, involves more than legal or managerial delegation of responsibility. It implies that a manager's subordinates acknowledge his or her ability. The basic criterion of authority, then, is acceptance by the group over which the authority is exercised. Authority is real only when subordinates *are willing to accept it.* Once your subordinates are no longer willing to accept your authority you're in trouble! Strikes, slowdowns, temporary work stoppages, excessive absenteeism, high turnover rates, poor morale, increased transferring out, increased scrap and rework, and countless other problems may well indicate to a manager or the organization that authority is being challenged, questioned, or disregarded.

Types of authority

Let us examine several fundamental types of individual authority that exist in our contemporary work world.

1. *Achieved authority* comes to individuals after they have met particular requirements, and is usually based on demonstrated competence.

2. *Ascribed authority* is arbitrarily assigned to an individual irrespective of accomplishment, competence, or desire.

3. *Personal authority* depends upon acceptance, but is generally based on personal qualities and attributes such as skills, character, appearance, personality, age, and success, to mention a few. Personal authority and the respect subordinates exhibit toward it develop over long periods of time out of acceptable interactions and interrelationships established between the authority-exerciser (the manager) and the authority-accepter (the subordinate).

4. *Technical authority* is a relatively new type of authority. It came into existence after the end of World War II and is the direct result of the proliferation of our vast technical competence. As an example, the acceptance and growth of the computer and its benefits to all types of organizations have literally lifted data processing managers into positions of authority they might never have reached otherwise had they selected some other field of endeavor. Electronics, chemistry, medicine, and certain specialized forms of engineering have created an array of new technical authority positions.

5. *Third-party intervention authority* is a form of group authority that has developed and expanded since the end of World War II. There are two large and massive third-party intervention groups that managers must acknowledge today, of which the first and foremost is government. Government intervention at all levels has been well recognized and has become a part of many managers' lives during the past 30 years. It is probably the most pervasive form of authority known today. Governmental exercise of authority is both subtle and direct, and its influence is so widespread that few, if any, enterprising

organizations and their managements have escaped its dominance. To assume an indifferent posture toward government intervention spells doom.

Organized labor unions comprise the second type of third-party intervention authority. To some managers this classification may be misleading since many enterprises operate entirely without organized labor. But those managers who work in a union-oriented organization must learn all they can about the labor movement and labor laws. In particular, they must know the labor contract under which they function. I am appalled, time and again, at the number of first-line supervisors and middle managers who lack such understanding.

Achieved, ascribed, and personal authority have been part of man's work history for centuries—the Old Testament is proof of that. But today's successful managers must also learn and understand the ramifications of the newer types of authority (technical and third-party intervention) that have developed in the last 30 years. It is this type of authority that presents the true challenge to becoming a successful manager in our contemporary work society.

Using successful authority techniques

After this brief introduction to some fundamental and identifiable kinds of authority found in our contemporary work world, let's examine techniques used by successful managers in four different situations.

WHEN YOU ARE THE NEW MANAGER

I have counseled, trained, and consulted with many young managers fresh out of training programs. My most significant bit of advice to them has always been the same, and it works: *Ask questions!*

Never hesitate to seek advice from superiors, peer group members, and subordinates. After all, they know that you're "new" in the game and you don't know very much about the intricacies of the job. By asking questions about the job, you are indirectly sharing your responsibilities and authority with others, and you will find that others are eager to help you, especially your subordinates. The success of this technique is primarily dependent upon the type of questions you ask, the information you seek, and especially the manner in which you ask it. Asking too many questions that are considered superficial or irrelevant by your subordinates may well be interpreted as a sign of indecision, weakness, or insecurity on your part. Once you get on top of the job and learn the basics, the frequency of asking questions will rapidly decline.

When addressing subordinates you might phrase a question like this: "If you were in my position, what would you do?" Or, "Why do *we* do it this way?" That question produces results. Some subordinates not only tell you how the job should be done, but tell you how they would do it if they were the boss, and still others, time permitting, would tell you their life history.

It is important, however, not to ask questions of subordinates that make you seem naive or lacking in self-confidence. Such questions as, "What do I do now?" or, "I am really unsure of myself, what should I do next?" immediately label you as an inexperienced, meek, and credulous manager who lacks self-assurance. One other point: Questions that stress "we" or "you" indicate to others their personal involvement and a willingness on your part to share your authority. Questions structured with the personal pronoun "I" sometimes tend to be interpreted as selfish and indicative of an unwillingness to share authority and responsibility with others.

Several years ago I was promoted to a front-line supervisor in a steel-producing division of a major steel firm. My basic indoctrination and supervisory orientation period lasted exactly *four hours,* So for several weeks I asked questions until I gained some degree of stability and confidence about the job—not about myself. I had no doubts about my own ability. But I also knew I had to learn as much as I could about the flow of work, its interrelationship with the other departments, and most important, the subordinates who did the actual work. Authority was the furthest thing from my thoughts and actions during that time. I knew if I pulled rank excessively and repeatedly with my subordinates, the next time I asked a question I would not receive an answer, or at best an "I don't know."

During those early weeks and months I found that I didn't have to exercise my authority in a hard-nosed fashion. Remarkable? Not quite. There were plenty of times I had to change orders or schedules

and work around breakdowns and delays, but I learned that my predecessor had been a very domineering supervisor who shouted at his
men and blamed them when things went wrong. Once I had learned
this, I could capitalize on his past mistakes.

Simply stated, I treated my subordinates with respect, indirectly
sharing my authority and responsibility with them by asking questions, and thanking them for their advice and help. I accepted them
for what they were and hoped they would accept me in like manner.
Recognizing that my performance could be measured only by the
quality of the work of my men, I was able to survive those early,
challenging managerial days.

In summary, the following points should be emphasized concerning successful authority techniques the new manager might use:

1. Ask those questions that elicit the answers you need, but do so
   in a manner that involves others' contributions and implies a
   willingness to share your authority.
2. Avoid the egotistical pronouns "I" or "me" when seeking information from subordinates. Respect, confidence, and teamwork
   are fundamentally built on the pronouns "we," "us," and
   "our."
3. Every job, regardless of rank or status, has a certain degree of
   responsibility built into it. For new managers it is totally impossible to know immediately as much about each subordinate's job as the subordinate knows about it. Therefore, by
   asking information-seeking questions rather than making
   demands, you quickly learn the degree of responsibility inherent in each job without losing your own status.
4. Find out as much as you can about your predecessor. Build
   your career by avoiding his or her weak points. How? Ask
   questions.

WHEN YOU UTILIZE THE NATURAL LEADER

Every work group of significant size develops its own natural or
informal leader. This is true of both union and nonunion work groups.
Identifying the natural leader is quite easy once you know what to
look for. Natural leaders come in all shapes and sizes, so don't look for
the biggest, tallest, or best-looking male or female. Many times the

natural leader will come forward and express to you, in public or private, the real feelings, reactions, and attitudes of the group. He or she is the one individual that members of the group seek out when they wish to discuss problems about work or their personal life. Normally, the majority of the group members support natural leaders and will defend them when verbally attacked by an outsider or another member of the group.

A natural leader can subtly or very vociferously control the work group's attitudes toward you. He or she can support you or impair your plans or aspirations. Usually, but not always, this individual has a good work record and has accumulated some degree of significant time, tenure, or seniority within a work unit or department. In some cases, the natural leader may enjoy more respect and confidence from the group membership than does the formal manager.

The natural leader is one of the key factors in almost all communication processes between the members of a designated work group. Individuals usually seek their advice, which is a reinforcement of the recognized position the natural leader has achieved. At times, the natural leader may come to you with special requests for other group members or the whole group. Some natural leaders are so proficient in their role that they actually possess informal authority. They can dispense appropriate rewards and punishment to other members without concern for recriminations from formal management individuals or other group members.

The natural leader gains that position as the result of group interaction and a natural selection process. Such informally achieved authority has been bestowed upon the natural leader by the majority of their group members. Although this achieved authority is very limited and lacks permanency, it is sometimes more powerful in getting or preventing group cooperation than the ascribed or assigned authority of a recognized formal member of management. Such a situation could well set the stage for a major confrontation between a manager and the natural leader. I have had the unhappiness of witnessing a few encounters of this nature, and while the formal manager won the battle on the surface, he lost the war in the long run. How, then, can managers utilize the natural leader and effectively exercise their own authority?

You have three alternative techniques at your disposal: do nothing and take your chances; create reciprocal relationships between yourself and the natural leader by making political side deals; or build a substantial relationship between yourself and the natural leader based on respect and consideration. The first two techniques can be successful, but only to a limited degree, while the third choice offers greatest potential. It's much cleaner; it's aboveboard; and in the long run (three to six months) the natural leader soon realizes that your authority is consistently exercised and fairly administered to both himself and others. The natural leader realizes from personal experience that sometimes you're going to be "damned if you do, and damned if you don't," when it comes to making decsisions and exercising your authority.

A "consciousness of kind" exists between you and the natural leader which is based on mutual empathy that stems from recognizing each other's important similarities of leadership behavior, the role of authority, and the sometimes frustrating consequences of playing the role of a manager.

To summarize the successful techniques in dealing with a natural leader:

1. Learn to identify who the natural leader is in your work group.
2. Build a wholesome relationship between yourself and the natural leader based on respect, consideration, fair play, and consistency when exercising your authority. This applies to other members of the work group as well as the natural leader.
3. Utilize natural leaders by periodically seeking their advice on minor work issues or impending organizational changes. Many times natural leaders can serve as a barometer of the attitudes and feelings of the work group. Do not, however, manipulate the natural leader for expediency's sake, or develop "political deals" based on reciprocal relationships or unofficial tradeoffs.

WHEN YOU ARE THE TECHNICAL MANAGER

Our industrial society has become increasingly specialized in the past 20 years because of the rapid growth and acceptance of technological innovations and applications. Few technical managers are "home-grown" products of the organizations in which they are presently employed. Financial experts, tax accountants, data processing managers, industrial hygienists, environmentalists, specialized chemists, and electronics engineers, to mention a few, are usually recruited away from their original training grounds and transplanted into new managerial roles immediately or within a short period of time.

Because of the need to incorporate technological innovations or to adhere to new governmental legislation or new labor contract administration, your organization may have placed you in a managerial position with little or no training in how to exercise your newly ascribed authority. Others within an organization, who might have been bypassed for the promotion, may feel resentful toward you. At any rate, you cannot hope to avoid exercising your authority by cloaking decisions in the mantle of expertise. This process becomes threadbare in a short period of time.

What successful authority techniques, then, can you effectively use? Obviously, in-house training and development courses are useful, but they require much of a manager's time and practice to become effective. A more expedient technique to use is the employment of the very skills that brought you to this level. Your subordinates are going to test your technical expertise sooner or later by subtle or direct means, if for no other reason than to make a subjective assessment of your qualifications. At this point you have a choice of three courses of action to follow.

First, demonstrate your technical expertise before they challenge or test you. Second, wait until your subordinates begin to probe for weak spots in your armor and then demonstrate your expertise. Third, and this must be done very early after your promotion, privately review all the personnel records of your subordinates to learn about their expertise. After a quick review, call each member of the group into your office individually, and, with discretion and candor, show your awareness of their backgrounds and seek the member's help and support in the future. There's nothing in the world that subordinates enjoy more than to be acknowledged by their boss as an important contributor to the success of the organization in the future. The simple fact is that we all love to be recognized. May I caution you, however, to conduct your reviews in such a manner that they are not interpreted as prying or invading privacy.

The very fact that you possess the authority to view their person-nel records and they cannot review yours is a sophisticated and unob-trusive manner of displaying your authority. Also the fact that you asked for their help and support leaves them no other choice but to give it to you. To do otherwise would be tantamount to rebellion. Of the three choices, I have found this third technique to be most effec-tive. The first technique, if carried to extremes, may be perceived as exhibitionism or showing off, and pity the poor subordinate who limps away from the encounter with a bloodied and bruised ego. The second technique may inadvertently expose you to some silly aca-demic or technical discussion which eventually ends in a draw, but permits the subordinate to walk away having the feeling of a moral victory over you. It's not what he or she thinks has been won that counts, it's feeling you have lost that really matters!

To summarize:

1. Avoid hiding behind your technical expertise in the hope that this will carry you through the early trial periods of your newly ascribed authority.
2. By personally and privately recognizing and acknowledging your subordinates' technical expertise, and by sincerely asking for their help and support, you create respect for yourself and confidence in those you are about to manage.
3. Above all, avoid direct antagonistic skirmishes with individuals who are bent on publicly testing your knowledge, expertise, or qualifications. Remember, even the janitor can teach you how to mop a floor.

WHEN YOU ARE THE OUTSIDE-RECRUITED MANAGER

The manager who was recruited from outside the organization is initially viewed as a stranger by the subordinates he or she will man-age, and there's a natural tendency to try to secure acceptance in the new group. Outside-recruited managers tend to bring with them the various managerial traits, behavior patterns, and experiences they learned in their former organization. They may not at first be com-pletely accepted by others.

Peer group members and especially subordinates will probe to determine similarities of nationality, education, religion, social or fraternal memberships, management philosophies, and even common personal interests, such as hobbies. Constant probing by others provides you with the opportunity to probe back and collect data that can be useful in the future. The exchange, however, is really unfair, because you can take distinct advantage of your position and authority by probing and seeking information at a ratio of ten to one or better.

Subordinates are somewhat hesitant to probe for information lest they seem to be snooping, and generally they respect your office or position. However, they are exceedingly willing to give more than they receive. If they should press too hard, you can skillfully turn them off because the authority you possess gives you license to do so.

The type and content of questions you ask can be interpreted by others to indicate your future asset or liability to the group. Thus, you are a stranger only to the degree that you may or may not share the same basic sentiments and values of the work group. You are rated by members of the group as an asset or a liability according to how they initially judge you to be a future help or hindrance in promoting the work group's values. Either to expose yourself completely at the beginning of a new assignment in order to gain quick acceptance or to be aloof in order to escape from the role of stranger may have profoundly negative consequences later on, especially when you are required to exercise your authority.

To summarize:

1. Both you and others are strangers to each other, and only time and the manner in which you administer authority will shorten or lengthen the social distance that exists.

2. Obviously you must permit others to probe into your personal life and managerial style to some degree, but take skillful advantage of your position by probing back at a ratio that's decidedly in your favor.

3. Remember, you're a stranger only to the degree that you share or do not share the same basic feelings and values of the group you must manage. To sustain a stranger role long after your recruitment is to handicap yourself severely.

YOUR AUTHORITY CHECKLISTS

The three checklists on authority that follow are presented to show that managerial authority in our contemporary work society is a two-way process. It starts with your superior's giving orders to you, and extends to your acceptance and execution of these orders by translating them into orders to your subordinates, who in turn are expected to accept and execute these same orders.

There are no "right" or "wrong" answers to any of the questions used in the checklists. *The intent is to stimulate you to think about your managerial role in authority.* How you perceive authority may well determine your present and future success as a manager.

Instructions. Read each question carefully. Apply the content and meaning of each question to your managerial style. Above all, be honest with yourself when administering the ratings. Use only one checkmark for each question.

PART ONE: HOW WELL DO YOU ACCEPT YOUR SUPERIOR'S AUTHORITY?

It is assumed that you, as a manager, report to an immediate superior who has more authority than you and who is responsible for directing, planning, organizing, and controlling many of your activities and functions.

	Always	Sometimes	Never
1. Do you feel you do an effective job in carrying out your superior's orders?	—	—	—
2. If for some reason you do not thoroughly understand an order to you from your superior, do you ask questions to clarify specific issues involved in the directive?	—	—	—
3. If there is a sincere difference of opinion between you and your superior on *how* an order is to be carried out, would you tell your boss?	—	—	—

4. Have you ever felt that your superior should carry out an order himself

	Always	Sometimes	Never
rather than give that responsibility to you?	—	—	—
5. If there is a sincere difference of opinion between you and your superior on *why* an order is to be carried out, would you tell your boss?	—	—	—
6. Are you aware of the parameters of authority you possess in the function of your job?	—	—	—
7. Are you willing to accept additional authority from your superior?	—	—	—
8. If there is a sincere difference of opinion between you and your superior on *when* an order is to be carried out, would you tell your boss?	—	—	—
9. Does your superior make an effort to understand and improve your shortcomings when you are having problems exercising your authority?	—	—	—
10. When you are given an order and accept authority from your superior, you do so for which of the following reasons?	—	—	—
a. I'm afraid of the consequences to me personally.	—	—	—
b. I'm afraid of the consequences to the organization.	—	—	—
c. I feel respect for my superior.	—	—	—
d. I know it's expected of me.	—	—	—
e. I feel it's a challenge.	—	—	—
f. I enjoy carrying out orders and exercising my authority.	—	—	—

PART TWO: HOW WELL DO YOU EXERCISE YOUR AUTHORITY?

In this checklist you are to review each question in terms of your specific managerial role and how you perceive the manner in which you exercise your authority.

	Always	Sometimes	Never
1. Do you feel you have the respect and confidence of your subordinates so that they honor your authority?	—	—	—
2. Do your subordinates know the parameters of your authority?	—	—	—
3. Do you make a conscientious effort to improve the exercising of your authority?	—	—	—
4. Do you use discipline as a constructive tool?	—	—	—
5. Do you stay within the limits of your assigned authority?	—	—	—
6. Do you help your subordinates improve their job competence?	—	—	—
7. Do you ever delegate your authority to your subordinates?	—	—	—
8. Has your authority ever been challenged by an employee or group of employees?	—	—	—
9. Are you willing to compromise your authority when dealing with managers on your level?	—	—	—
10. Do you believe that exercising authority is a learned behavior pattern rather than an inborn trait?	—	—	—

PART THREE: HOW WELL DO YOUR SUBORDINATES ACCEPT YOUR AUTHORITY?

Now that you have completed two checklists concerning authority—your acceptance of your superior's authority, and how you exercise your authority—complete the third checklist on how you feel your subordinates accept your authority.

	Always	Sometimes	Never
1. Do you feel your subordinates do an effective job in carrying out your orders?	—	—	—
2. Would you say that your em-			

	Always	Sometimes	Never
ployees are willing to accept additional authority from you?	—	—	—
3. Do your employees ever request you to clarify a specific order?	—	—	—
4. Has an employee said that he or she would carry out an order, and failed to do so?	—	—	—
5. Have you ever had an employee refuse to carry out an order?	—	—	—
6. Has an employee ever challenged your authority?	—	—	—
7. Has an employee ever told you, "That's not my job!"	—	—	—
8. Do you feel that training employees to become more competent on their jobs makes it easier for them to accept your authority?	—	—	—
9. Do you feel that if you demonstrate sincere respect for your employees they will in turn respect you, and as a result accept your authority more readily?	—	—	—
10. When your employees are given an order and accept your authority, they do so for which of the following reasons?			
a. They fear they'll be disciplined.	—	—	—
b. They are worried about the consequences to the organization.	—	—	—
c. They don't know any better.	—	—	—
d. They respect you.	—	—	—
e. It's part of their job.	—	—	—
f. That's what they're paid to do.	—	—	—
g. They have no other choice.	—	—	—

How did you do? There's a total of 43 questions in these 3 checklists. If you checked off more than 10 "Never" answers you need help in shaping your attitudes toward authority, or in sharpening your techniques for exercising it.

2 FACE-TO-FACE COMMUNICATION

The Basic Interaction Process

Communication is a basic process of interaction between people who are both transmitters and recipients of information. Thousands of books and articles have been written about this subject. The discussion in this chapter, however, will concern only the following areas: the oral communication process, listening, the grapevine, communicating with your superior, those pregnant pronouns, and body language. Various successful techniques will be presented as an aid in making you a better communicator.

I have avoided the broad area of written communication in this chapter in order to concentrate on the more numerous face-to-face oral exchanges enacted daily. Memos, letters, notices, and written policies and procedures lack the emotions, feelings, and facial and body expressions that dominate oral communications. Written communications tend to be formal, stiff, and indirect, and present few techniques useful for rebutting, challenging, or otherwise engaging in direct interaction with others.

The oral communication process

Over the years specialists in semantics and interpersonal communications have consistently shown the complexity of this process and have identified the roadblocks that alter or distort both oral and written communications. Whenever you communicate orally with another individual, there are 10 different mental processes or steps involved in each single transaction. Here is an example of a very simple oral exchange that illustrates the 10 processes that take place between two people.

The manager, Mr. Jones, comes into the office at the beginning of the day and greets his secretary, Ms. Smith.

What you *mean* to say . . .
"Good morning, Ms. Smith."
What you *actually* said . . .
"Good morning, Ms. Smith."
What you *think* the other person heard . . .
Mr. Jones to himself—"I think she heard me say, 'Good morning, Ms. Smith.' "
What the other person *thinks* she heard . . .
Ms. Smith to herself—"What did he say?
I think he said, 'Good morning, Ms. Smith.' "
What the other person *actually* heard . . .
"Good morning, Ms. Smith."

Then Ms. Smith replies:

What the other person *means* to say . . .
"Good morning, Mr. Jones."
What the other person *actually* said . . .
"Good morning, Mr. Jones."
What the other person *thinks* you heard . . .
Ms. Smith to herself—"Gosh, I think he heard me say, 'Good morning, Mr. Jones.' "
What the other person *thinks* he heard . . .
Mr. Jones to himself—"Did she say 'Good morning' to me?"
What the other person *actually* heard . . .
"Good morning, Mr. Jones."

Is the above superficial example somewhat confusing? Perhaps, but imagine how complex a lengthy discussion can become when a manager is discussing job performance with an employee. Successful managers know that it pays to be aware of the distortions that arise in oral communications. Many managers who believe themselves to be effective communicators expect their subordinates to behave in predictable fashion. In fact, however, the only assurance in good communications is that the persons involved in the interacting process comprehend what each is trying to communicate. A loyal subordinate can understand perfectly well what his or her boss is communicating and still fail to carry out the actions requested. As a rule, however, when good comprehension takes place in the communication process, effective job performance results. The following successful techniques should help you develop better communication skills.

Listening as a technique

What's the difference between hearing and listening? Hearing is done with the ears only, whereas listening is done with both the ears and mind. Hearing is usually taken for granted, as a mere matter of sound waves bouncing off the inner ear receiving devices. Listening, on the other hand, is a skill that requires effort, empathy, and a complete comprehension of the message.

NONDIRECTIVE LISTENING TECHNIQUE

When communicating with subordinates, a manager can control the conversation by speaking most of the time and by continually asking questions that prevent an open discussion. Managers who use this approach should not be surprised to discover that they learn little about employees' attitudes or their feelings or problems within the organization.

A more successful technique is the nondirective listening approach, in which the manager uncovers the subordinate's feelings by letting him or her do most of the talking and by using open-ended questions that encourage further discussion. Here are the essential components of nondirective listening that managers must learn and practice:

1. *Give full attention to your employees when they are speaking to you.* If possible, maintain good eye contact. Often the eyes say more than the words.

2. *Use open-ended questions to keep the discussion moving.* Avoid using questions that simply require a yes or no answer. For example, a direct question might be: "Did you tell her to type that report?" A nondirective question on the same subject might be structured this way: "What did you tell her about typing that report?" Frequently the first words of a nondirective question may start off like this: "You feel that. . . ."

3. *Learn to use feedback listening.* This technique consists of repeating in slightly different language what the other person has just said. For example, your subordinate has just told you: "I don't think she did a good job typing that report." Your response should be structured so as to encourage the person to continue expressing his or her thoughts so that you find out the reasons for the statement. You might reply by saying: "You feel she didn't do a good job on that report?" This technique helps to verify your understanding of what your subordinate said and encourages the employee to continue the discussion, which may uncover other feelings or additional information.

4. *Make use of silence during a conversation.* During long conversations, brief periods of silence occur. Try to refrain from speaking during a pause. Wait out the other person. Silence on the subordinate's part may mean that he or she is not sure whether or not to tell you something more. When you remain silent, the subordinate may choose to reinforce previous statements and offer additional information.

5. *Avoid showing approval or disapproval.* Many times managers have an unconscious tendency to show approval or disapproval of what an employee is saying through their eye contact or by simple facial expressions. This should be avoided. If necessary, look away from the individual who is speaking to you and maintain a solemn "poker face."

It's much easier to describe these listening techniques than it is to put them into practice. As a manager, you have the right to manipulate certain conversations with your subordinates. To do it successfully you must learn to listen and practice the above techniques. There are critical times in every manager's job when it is necessary to have specific information in order to make the best decisions possible. By learning and practicing these listening techniques, your communication style comes across as genuine and implies concern and interest to those you work with. Remember, listening is the key to successful communication.

HOW AND WHEN TO STOP LISTENING

Listening pays off. But there are also situations when listening is simply a waste of time. Below are four short successful techniques that you should use when you feel it's time to stop listening and get on with more important matters.

Getting back on the track. You're sitting in a conference attended by four or five other managers who are trying to map out a strategy to solve a problem. Soon the subject gets sidetracked into some irrelevant area which seems to have more temporary appeal. Before you know it, individual personalities or interdepartmental conflicts enter the discussion. Whether or not you're the chairman of the group, simply cut short this ineffective dialogue and get the discussion back on the track. You'll probably not win a popularity contest for this maneuver, but your time is too valuable to waste.

Giving a fast answer. You're rushed for time, but an employee comes up to you with a problem. You permit the employee to state the problem, and the solution is obvious to you. You realize that the employee is looking for an answer based on your knowledge and experience. Instead of letting the employee systematically work out the solution by a series of deductive questions and answers, give him or her a precise, firm answer. You might also encourage employees to consider using the same solution in the future. You'll save their time and yours, provide them with a possible model solution, and leave them with a feeling of genuine interest and concern.

Stopping gossip. You're in your office one day and an employee comes in and volunteers to tell you a story concerning another employee. It doesn't take you long to realize that the employee is committing character assassination of a fellow worker. Stop it right then and there and tell the individual that you are doing so. Continuing to listen makes you an accessory to the fact and a party to the assassination. To continue the dialogue only encourages the employee to do it again later on because he or she knows it's possible to get your ear. Furthermore, if you fall for this manipulative device, the employee expects you to take some kind of action with the other employee. An employee who is encouraged to talk about fellow employees behind their backs will probably do the same to you.

Shooting questions. Another manager sitting in your office has been carrying on a meandering monologue for over 10 minutes about a recurring common problem. You've been down this road before, and the monologue is not only boring, but a waste of time. The best thing to do is orally "belt" the other manager with a couple of rapid-fire questions as you get up to leave your office. This immediately stops the monologue and makes the other manager think through the problem.

The grapevine

Groups arise and persist in work organizations only because they satisfy the social, economic, and psychological needs of their members. Therefore anything may be a need if it is so defined by the group. Thus informal organizations arise and are perpetuated within the formal organization because of the functions they serve. Once a group is established within an organization, and this includes management groups, it wants all the information that might affect its welfare either positively or negatively. When groups are not apprised of the policies, motives, and intentions behind *changes* in the organization, they become both anxious and suspicious. Changes that affect people, policy, methods, production, and pay scales are usually the most important situations that spawn rumors. Efforts are made to tap the formal lines of communication, and rumors spread like wildfire through the informal network of communications known as the grapevine.

The grapevine, intertwined throughout the entire organization, has four basic characteristics which managers must be aware of:

1. The information transmitted by it is usually distorted.
2. The speed with which information flows is very rapid.

3. The grapevine, as a process, is not responsible for the mistakes and untruths it produces.
4. It is very difficult to pin down the original source of its distortions.

Managers should learn to recognize these four characteristics in order to make the grapevine work in their favor.

SUCCESSFUL GRAPEVINE TECHNIQUES

The grapevine will always flourish in an active group of concerned employees. However, it is not the existence of the grapevine, but what a manager does with it that matters.

When an employee relates a rumor to you about some change that is supposed to take place which you haven't heard about before, there are several courses of action you can take:

Deny the rumor.

Seek additional information about the rumor from the employee.

Casually admit you've heard the rumor but haven't had a chance to substantiate the facts.

Admit that you've heard the rumor, then add a different item to the story in an effort to counteract it.

If you are aware of a change that is to take place, but you have been instructed by your superior to withhold information until a formal announcement is made, you can again use any of the four techniques. Not all the techniques bring benefits.

If you deny the rumor, you may be lying to a loyal employee, which saps one's own integrity and, from a practical point of view, vitiates trust. Because it's always helpful to have someone in your group relate information to you from time to time, it's inadvisable to use this technique.

Seeking additional information from a cooperative employee is a subtle way of learning which manager has leaked the information. Sometimes it is valuable to know which managers lack discretion, especially if you want to use the grapevine yourself. Some managers have difficulty adhering to their superior's directions to keep silent. In the long run this can be harmful to their careers.

By casually admitting that you have heard this rumor but haven't checked the facts, you're not lying to your loyal employee. Moreover, you can't be accused of leaking information if there's a massive investigation by top management to find the informant.

If you wish to counteract the rumor, make sure the item you convey strongly supports some facet of management's current philosophy and does not place you in the position of lying. You must keep those channels of informal communication open at all times.

An intelligent manager can often use the grapevine to spread information by translating the organization's more formal messages into language employees may better understand. A manager can thus convey specific information and detailed facts the formal communication system omitted. Facts are a manager's best remedy for rumors. By relating the facts of the situation to one reliable person, the manager is using the grapevine to his advantage, since he can count on that individual to tell many others.

It's important to keep in mind that some top managements purposely start rumors to measure employees reactions to proposed changes. This is known as "sending up a trial balloon." Depending upon the employees' reactions, they may reconsider, adjust, or delay their decisions about the proposed change. However, not all managements use this technique.

Keeping your boss well informed

As a manager you make decisions primarily on the basis of the information you receive from your employees. Every manager is also someone else's subordinate, so that everyone is involved in upward communications. A good manager also realizes that his boss cannot make sound executive decisions unless he or she knows everything that must be known. Likewise, as manager, you know that your boss is as accountable as you are, and that your boss must always be able to answer questions that someone above asks. In short, the experienced manager understands that one of the major responsibilities of being a manager is to keep the boss well informed.

EIGHT UPWARD COMMUNICATION TECHNIQUES TO USE

If you want to develop your upward communication skills, here are eight brief techniques to practice:

1. Report immediately any critical developments or changes in your area of responsibility.
2. Organize the information before you present it. Give priority to what is most important.
3. Give your superior the full story, if time permits.
4. Present facts, not your personal interpretation.
5. Report errors and mistakes in carrying out instructions that will affect job results. This is tough to do, but it's a mark of honesty on your part.
6. Keep your boss constantly informed about employees' attitudes, productivity, morale, or special problems.
7. Avoid passing on information based entirely on assumptions. If you don't know, say so.
8. Seek your boss's counsel on problems you're not sure how to handle. Experienced superiors will have more respect for your credibility because part of their responsibility is to help develop your skills and abilities.

SEVEN UPWARD COMMUNICATION TECHNIQUES TO AVOID

Organizations and jobs differ; conditions and situations vary; the timing of upward communications is not always controllable on your part; but most important, executives have their own personal receptivity and reactions to subordinate managers' communication processes. Because of this, there are certain self-development communication techniques one should *avoid* when keeping your boss informed.

1. Never lie to your boss. Never, never, never. If you've made a mistake, didn't know the answer, or botched an assignment, admit it! Once you lie, you have to keep on lying, and the emotional impact and unnecessary pressure you bring to bear on yourself are not worth the consequences.

2. Don't tell half the story or half-truths. These are as bad as outright lies. If you failed to investigate a problem, or failed to follow up on a problem, admit it. I have always found that the higher one advances in the hierarchy, the more proficient one becomes at protecting oneself when conflicting communications arise and someone has to pay the bill. If you're caught in a lie or half-truth, you and you alone pay the bill with compounded interest.

3. Don't censor upward communications. You're not doing your boss a favor by protecting him or her from unpleasant news. By censoring upward communications, you are in reality making your boss less effective, and if an immediate and important decision is required it could become costly to both of you.

4. Don't try to save face by overprotecting yourself. Managers who down-play certain facts which they feel reflect personal deficiencies may someday be questioned directly or indirectly about their competency.

5. Don't sell yourself short either. If your superior asks for any ideas you might have about a problem and you see a way of improving a procedure, method, or policy, tell your boss about it.

6. Don't avoid talking over a problem with your superior—that doesn't make it disappear. Avoiding or postponing discussions now can have serious consequences later.

7. Don't discuss solutions before you discuss the problem. That's putting the cart before the horse. State the problem first. Give your superior a chance to digest the ramifications of the problem. Let him or her ask questions about the problem, because the questions asked may suggest different or additional solutions to the problem. Moreover, you gain insight into how your supervisor normally approaches a problem. Finally, if you choose to discuss the solution before discussing the problem, your superior may wonder why you wasted everyone's time by discussing it at all.

Those pregnant pronouns

Pregnant pronouns are the personal pronouns, which are often emotionally charged and may lead to either favorable or unfavorable work behavior. "I" and "me," "you" and "we" can divide or unite, agitate or soothe, create harmonious relationships or produce harmful impressions. Managers should be very conscious of the selection and use of their pronouns when communicating up, down, or sideways. When used with psychological sensitivity, they can work miracles for you, but when used insensitively, they can fill others with misgivings. A good manager should want to control and encourage his or her subordinates into the most productive and efficient aspects of work they are capable of. The careful use of pronouns can help do this.

ME AND I

Careless use of the pronouns "I" and "me" can be devastating to a manager, especially if used in the wrong tone or with degrading emphasis when speaking to a subordinate. The following statement directed at a subordinate having difficulty with a machine could well turn off the employee's enthusiasm for doing the job:

"Are *you* having trouble again? Here, let *me* show *you* how *I* do it."

In this case the pronouns imply clumsiness or stupidity on the part of the subordinate. The same situation could be handled in this manner:

"Is that machine giving *you* trouble again? *It*'s a little tricky at times. Here's the way *I* do it. Now, shall *we* try it?" The pronouns in this instance refer to the complexities of the machine, and not the incompetence of the individual.

YOU AND YOURS

Watch how you use the pronoun *you*. It can separate a manager from an employee for a long period of time. For instance:

"*You*'ve slipped lately, Joe. *You* better get with it!" Statements like these can be chillingly brutal. The same situation could well be handled in this manner:

"Joe, *I've* noticed *your* performance lately. Let's see what *we* can do about it." In this situation, the use of *us* and *we* combines and unites the manager with his subordinate.

Body language—the nonverbal way to communicate

Do you know how to communicate by using body language? Do you understand what other people are communicating to you when they use body language? Actually, all of us communicate with one another nonverbally, and most of the time we're not aware that we're doing it. We gesture with our eyebrows, head, shoulders, and hands. Our eyes meet, then turn away, or we cross our legs and fold our arms, or we shift our body positions when sitting on a chair or couch. Most managers pay little heed to these forms of nonverbal communication. Others take them for granted and consider them incidental.

Today's managers, however, should become more aware of body language in order to help them gain a clearer understanding of another person's basic attitudes and reactions. And equally important, they should be aware of their own body language. Various gestures such as body movements, shoulder shrugs, mimicry, and facial expressions indicate certain messages when interacting with superiors and subordinates.

At this point the science of kinesics, the interpretations of body language, is in its infant stage. Obviously, some gestures have an understandable conscious meaning. For instance, a raised middle finger, or a quick grasp of the right bicep followed by the raising of the right forearm and clenched fist, convey hostility and insult. People often raise an eyebrow automatically to express surprise, and others unconsciously scratch their heads indicating bewilderment. We shrug our shoulders for indifference, wink an eye for intimacy, and tap our fingers for impatience.

Beyond these universal gestures are the more sophisticated and individually identifiable forms of nonverbal communication that managers should learn to look for. In particular, you should learn to identify consistent forms of body language used by your superior, and to interpret the meanings behind the use of these gestures. The intelligent manager knows that, as adults, we all tend to cloak our feelings and attitudes in polite words. But by studying your superior's body language, and knowing what it means, you can gain insight into your boss's personality, feelings, and attitudes that can be successfully used at some later and perhaps critical time. The more you know about your superior's body language patterns, the better you can predict his or her feelings and attitudes toward various issues in which you are involved.

It is extremely difficult to observe and interpret the body language of your boss when you are engaged in a conversation. Time and concentration on the oral part of the communications do not permit this. However, try to observe any foot or leg movement during the conversation—crossing and uncrossing of legs, for example, or foot tapping. These are signs of impatience. Observe what your boss does with his or her eyes, and notice hand, finger, or arm movements. If your superior rubs his or her nose, or gently strokes his or her chin with one hand, try to associate the gesture with what was just said. It could mean there is disagreement between you. Many times there appears to be a close correlation between the spoken word and the nonverbal body gesture.

One of the best times to learn to identify and interpret your superior's gestures is during a conference with other members of your department and your superior. The presence of the other members provides you with time and protection for your observations. Where you sit at the conference table is most important. For closeup observations of facial expressions, you may want to be next to your superior, but this makes it difficult to take notes. For an overall view, take a position furthest from the superior and off to one side of the table. Here you can observe both the superior and others in dialogue and occasionally jot down a note or two.

It takes a long time to identify the consistent forms of body language your superior uses and to interpret the meanings behind these gestures. One way to practice this technique is to turn on the television and omit the sound. The best type of programs to practice with are the soap operas and situation comedies. Soap operas are especially helpful because most of the actors tend to overplay their roles, and there are more closeups, with emphasis on eye and mouth movements to reinforce the action that takes place on a limited stage area. Situation comedies, on the other hand, tend to present more body movements to transmit to the audience the intended comedy or pathos in the script.

Another way to practice is to observe outstanding salespeople at work. You will notice that they are aware of many of the body language clues a client transmits. If you have the opportunity to discuss this matter with outstanding salespeople, they can point out certain standard gestures and movements to look for when selling a product or service to clients.

A MANAGER–EMPLOYEE COMMUNICATION CHECKLIST

The purpose of this brief checklist is as follows:

1. To briefly summarize various communication techniques presented in this chapter.

2. To encourage the reader to conduct a self-development exercise by checking off what you consider to be the most appropriate answer to each question.

3. To stimulate your thoughts about the communication techniques you presently use with your superiors and subordinates.

4. To inspire the reader to identify, learn, and experiment with new and different communication techniques in your present role as a manager.

Instructions. Read each question carefully. Apply the content and meaning of each question to your particular managerial life style. Be honest with yourself when administering the ratings. Use only one checkmark for each question.

	Always	Sometimes	Never
1. I try to keep from using the personal pronoun "I."	___	___	___
2. I consider myself to be a good listener.	___	___	___
3. I use nondirective listening techniques when discussing problems with my subordinates.	___	___	___
4. I am aware that semantic differences exist when I engage in a conversation.	___	___	___
5. During conversations with my subordinates I make use of silence to encourage the other person to keep talking.	___	___	___
6. I use reflective listening, that is, repeating back in slightly different language what the other person has just said.	___	___	___

	Always	Sometimes	Never
7. When conversing with my superior about a problem, I give him or her the facts.	——	——	——
8. In the early stages of a conversation with another individual I avoid showing approval or disapproval at what he or she is saying.	——	——	——
9. I use the grapevine to convey useful information and to translate the organization's formal messages in language employees may better understand.	——	——	——
10. I am aware of the various forms of body language my superiors and subordinates use when I am conversing with them.	——	——	——

Evaluation. How did you score? A predominant number of Always answers, with perhaps two or three Sometimes answers would indicate that you're a good to excellent communicator.

 **CONFLICT**

Management at Variance

Conflict is a social interaction process wherein two or more people or groups diverge or clash in their opinions or goals. It may be viewed as an extreme form of competition. Conflict, however, is not necessarily dysfunctional, because a certain amount of it is essential to group formation and the maintenance of work-group life.

While it is necessary to outline some of the causes of conflict, the main emphasis will concern the identification and use of successful management techniques to resolve these problems. These techniques include recognizing the differences between perception and opinion, handling differences of opinion, and resolving conflict problems. A checklist of these techniques concludes this chapter.

Causes of conflict

What are the causes of management conflict? There are probably as many causes of conflict in organizations as there are managements, but some of the major reasons are discussed below.

The organization of management. The divisions and specializations of management in our contemporary organizational hierarchies give rise to much managerial conflict.

Changing values within management ranks. Today, more middle managers openly question the authority and decisions of their superiors. This attitude, coupled with the feeling of being locked in and of having little chance for advancement, plus opportunities in other organizations, has increased independence among many middle managers. Obviously, such managerial changing values can lead to an increased frequency of conflict between middle managers and their superiors.

The unequal application of human relations. Increased emphasis on treating rank-and-file employees with respect for their rights has caused many managers to consider their own rights and privileges. Unfortunately, in our contemporary work world it's much easier to dismiss a manager than to fire a union employee. Consequently, the failure of higher management to consider the rights and privileges of subordinate managers is another source of conflict.

Line managers vs. staff managers. Fifty years ago this type of managerial conflict was unheard of. Today, line managers believe that staff managers are encroaching on their territory and taking away what remaining power and status they have. Thus conflicts arise as line managers fight back to protect their power and status.

Staff managers, on the other hand, complain of a lack of cooperation on the part of line managers. These specialists feel they are being ignored, or treated as inferior or parasitical, and subsequently release their anxieties against their counterparts, especially when cooperation is not forthcoming.

Line managers vs. line managers. Conflict between line managers occurs in several kinds of situations. Where shift or turn work is involved, one line manager blames the other for not producing equal units of production. When production quotas are not reached, production managers blame the maintenance manager for long unnecessary delays and breakdowns. Maintenance managers, on the other hand, retaliate by accusing production people of operating the equipment until it breaks down, or prohibiting them from exercising planned outages. Or in assembly-line production one unit in the line charges the preceding unit with slowing down, overproducing, or making poor-quality subassembled units that require rework.

Staff managers vs. staff managers. Staff managers' confrontations are less aggressive than line-staff, or line-line conflicts, and usually arise from a lack of cooperation or understanding. In extreme cases, staff-staff conflict can be the direct result of head-on collisions between department heads who are stubbornly rigid or overbearing. Staff managers often battle over a proper slice of the budget.

The urge to merge. Conflicts arise when two or more organizations merge. The assignment of positions and responsibility in the new structure causes concern and apprehension between managers and executives.

The never-ending struggle—managers vs. subordinates. The causes of conflict in this category are endless, and run the spectrum from personality clashes to resentment toward authority.

The individual manager vs. the organization. Do organizations stifle the creativity, individuality, and imagination of the American manager? Is there a conflict between the needs of the individual and the organization that employs him or her? These questions have been discussed at length over the past years. Generally speaking, organizations are many things to many managers. To an individual who seeks maximum fulfillment, they offer opportunity, material resources, and encouragement toward attaining these psychological goals and objectives. The individual who needs a relatively stable, well-structured, secure, and protective environment will also find satisfaction in the organization.

The individual inner conflicts of managers. When exercising power and authority, or when struggling with decisions concerning subordinates, or when inadvertently caught in organization crosscurrents, managers cannot escape the most critical conflicts of all: the conflicts which they harbor within.

Perception

Our attitudes, interests, goals, values, intelligence, power and authority, and personality all enter into how we perceive a situation, problem, or expectation. As a manager, you have probably learned that different perceptions by different managers, subordinates, and superiors have led to many misunderstandings that could have been avoided.

What basically causes different perceptions, and what can we do to understand them better? Part of the answer is contained in the fact that all people have a trait known as selective perception. That is, we hear what we want to hear, see what we want to see, and emotionally feel what we want to feel. Inherent in this trait is the ability to block out or ignore circumstances, situations, or problems that we feel will be harmful to us or will not fit into our scheme of things.

Let's examine a successful technique that might be helpful to you when you are trying to obtain mutual perception and avoid conflict.

HOW TO OBTAIN MUTUAL PERCEPTION

Let's assume that you're discussing a critical problem that exists between you and another manager. Both of you are on the same level with equal power, authority, and responsibility. During the discussion you realize that you might lose the issue, and the eventual outcome could lead to disagreement and possible conflict. This you want to avoid. Your goal is to have the problem resolved in your favor, and avoid disagreement and conflict, if possible. To do this you must expand and qualify the perceptions of both your counterpart and yourself. There are two questions that you should ask of the other manager at this point in the discussion, and the questions must be asked in this order:

Start by asking, "I wonder if I see this problem the same way you do?" By placing the pronoun "I" before "you" in the question, you appear to be acquiescing to your opponent, that is, submitting to his or her requests. However, this is not your purpose. What you're really trying to do is to understand how your opponent perceives the problem. This subtle manipulative technique often brings out in the open the real underlying reasons for the position of the other manager.

If the other manager is not aggressively overbearing, or stubborn, he or she will usually react by repeating the same position, often with additional details to reinforce it and to bring your understanding into closer accord with his or her own. This response automatically gives you a greater insight into his or her real purpose, and perhaps provides you with a better perception of the problem as the other manager sees it. How you respond depends on what has been said, and whether you're willing to accept this information, to compromise, or to continue the discussion.

Therefore, the second question may or may not be necessary. If you feel it is, then ask: "I wonder if you see this problem the same way I do?" You have switched the personal pronouns so that the emphasis is placed on the other person—he or she is directly asked to acquiesce to your position. The second question is psychologically fair and equitable, because you yielded, or appeared to yield your position, in the first question. This question could be the decisive or turning point for both of you in the discussion. What you hope to accomplish now is to get the other manager to understand how you perceive the problem. Assume the discussion continues after you have shared perceptions and additional information. If a definitive agreement has not been reached, you both have three choices remaining:

1. You may each maintain your positions, which will lead to disagreement and possible conflict.
2. One of you may submit to the other's request and avoid disagreement and conflict.
3. You may both agree to compromise your positions, since this would be best for the organization and for each of you.

In taking the initiative in asking these questions, you may tip the balance in your favor, and you may not. If you do not reach an understanding, suggest that both of you temporarily table the issue, so that additional thought can be given to the problem, and schedule a future meeting to discuss the matter.

PERCEPTIONS AND RESISTANCE TO CHANGE

Employees' attitudes toward management in general, and their managers in particular, will often determine how they interpret a situation. Resistance to change, for example, is frequently based on a mistrust of management rather than on objective evaluations of the change itself. How subordinates perceive change will depend on how the change will affect them personally, or how they perceive the motives of the organization, or how they perceive the motives of their manager.

If employees feel personally threatened, or are suspicious of the motives underlying the change, conflict is bound to take place. This type of resistance and conflict usually arises because of poor communications on management's part. How does a manager avoid creating mistrust amongst his subordinates, especially when a major change is to take place?

There are basically two types of changes we should consider. First are changes that affect subordinates in a positive, helpful, and rewarding manner. These are pay raises, additional fringe benefits, promotions, or organizational growth. Obviously, these types of changes are seldom resisted. The second type of change, however, is viewed as a personal threat to an employee, and involves pay reductions, demotions, workforce reductions, and terminations. These are trauma situations and are met with resistance and low morale; in extreme cases they create aggressive conflicts toward management, if mishandled by managers. The absolutely toughest job a manager has to experience in his career is terminating the services of a good employee because of cutbacks.

The leveling technique, discussed below, tells you how to avoid mishandling major changes, and how to reduce employee resistance and conflict.

The leveling technique. Leveling is simply a straightforward, nononsense communication process—"telling it like it is." In management, it is the art of truthfully informing one's subordinates of upcoming changes that will directly affect them and their jobs. Facts relating to the changes are presented and the reasons given. Discussions that follow are directed toward an objective evaluation of the change. Questions are encouraged and fielded by the manager with candor and simplicity.

This is a difficult technique to use whenever the forthcoming changes threaten subordinates' jobs and their security. Some managers overplay their role when using this technique because of their sympathy for their employees. Other managers try to get it over with as fast as they can because of the distastefulness of the assignment. Thus, they pay little attention to encouraging questions, or to presenting objective evaluations resulting from the change.

Whether you're successful in totally avoiding conflict remains to be seen at some time in the future. However, if managers follow the simple procedural steps of this leveling technique, rather than either over- or underplaying this assignment, they cannot be accused of mishandling a major negative change. As an employee once told me after he was informed that he was going to be laid off, "There's not much I can do about the layoff, but what gripes me is the way they [management] went about telling me!"

PERCEPTION FILTERS

A manager's evaluation of his or her subordinates is based on what I call perception filters. For example, if a manager likes an employee, for whatever reason, the manager will overlook certain delinquent or negative aspects of the employee's work performance, personality, age, dress, appearance, or attitudes, so long as the employee gets the job done. A different manager may be too negative about the same employee regardless of whether the employee gets the job done. Or consider the situation of a salesperson who constantly meets his or her sales quotas, but engages in after-hours socializing and drinking with the clients. One sales manager overlooks the after-hours affairs because of the salesperson's outstanding performance, whereas a different sales manager makes an issue of these extracurricular activities regardless of the outstanding sales performance. Two different sales managers are using two different sets of perception filters in assessing the same employee. One sales manager is filtering out the so-called negatives, while the second is filtering in the negatives and interpreting them as detrimental.

At this point you may ask, Which manager is right and which manager is wrong? Rightness and wrongness are irrelevant. The real question should be, What type of perception filter do you use when dealing with your subordinates? The following questions may serve you as a technique for properly adjusting your perception filters when dealing with subordinates.

1. Have I considered the employee's background and how it may influence his or her work performance? (This is especially important today because of the increased numbers of females, minorities, and younger employees entering the labor market.)
2. Do I recognize that he or she may have needs and values that are different from mine?
3. How are my needs and values as a manager influencing the manner in which I perceive this employee?
4. How are the needs and values of the department or organization influencing the manner in which I perceive this employee?

After asking yourself these four questions you might suggest that your subordinate ask the following questions of himself or herself:

1. Have I considered my manager's background and how it may influence his or her expectations of me?
2. Do I recognize that my manager may have needs and values that are different from mine?
3. How are my needs and values as an employee influencing the manner in which I see and understand my manager?
4. How are the needs and values of the department or organization influencing the manner in which I see or understand my manager?

To carry this technique to its end point, you might ask the employee to tell you his or her individual answers to each of these four questions. Listen carefully, then restate the answers to the employee in your own language. Next, request the employee to listen to your individual answers to each of your four questions. Have the employee restate each answer back to you in his or her own language. This technique brings out the perceptual differences between you and your employee concerning a problem or critical situation. Granted, this is not an easy technique to use, but it will help both you and your employee to understand each other's perceptions and settle disagreements before they become conflicts.

Projection

Another cause of disagreement and conflict that can arise between a manager and his or her superiors, peer group members, or subordinates resulting from differing perceptions is a psychological process known as projection. Projection is a defense mechanism people use to avoid anxiety and threats to their self-esteem. It is a way of rejecting an unwanted aspect of oneself by attributing it to others. For instance, a manager who feels anxious or perhaps guilty about a problem may try to rid himself of these feelings by attributing them to someone else. In this way, a manager may satisfy, to some degree, a need for emotional release, thus decreasing guilt feelings or pent-up frustrations.

Another form of projection is the assumption that others have the same attitudes, needs, or characteristics as oneself. When this assumption is proved wrong, the result is often conflict based on misunderstanding. Some years ago I conducted a study at a large chemical company in Pittsburgh, Pennsylvania.* I surveyed over 300 employees, who made up 22 distinct and identifiable groups within 5 different levels of the organization. I found that certain motivational factors were related to the level in the hierarchy in which individuals normally work.

For example, the lower-level, nonmanagement individuals ranked wages, security, and working conditions as most important. Management personnel in the higher levels of the hierarchy ranked achievement, promotions, and recognition as their most important motivators. Thus, these findings indicated to me that managers in the higher levels of the organization who indulged in projecting their motivational efforts upon their subordinates at the lower levels were totally ineffective. Simply stated, managers who try to project their needs upon their subordinates are creating conflicts, because subordinates' needs are different from theirs. This is why we sometimes hear managers make such statements as, "I can't understand my employees; they don't seem to have any interest in their jobs!" Or another state-

*Paul W. Cummings, "Does Herzberg's Theory Really Work?" *The Personnel Administrator*, October 1974, pp. 19–23.

ment often heard is, "The more you give these people, the more they want!"

A SIMPLE EMPLOYEE SURVEY TECHNIQUE

Here's a survey technique you might want to use with a group of your employees to measure the differences between your values and needs and those of your subordinates.

1. Make up a one-page survey form as illustrated below.
2. Pass out one form to each employee.
3. Request that they fill out the form and return it to you. (Employees' names are not required.)
4. Administer the survey to yourself.
5. Summarize the group's total responses.
6. Compare the group's responses to your own.
7. Note any differences and similarities.

AN EMPLOYEE SURVEY

Listed below are 10 items employees consider to be important to their jobs. Read the descriptions of the items first, then rank them in the order of importance to you. *Do not assign the same number to any two items.* The most important item to you should be ranked number 1, and the least important item should be ranked number 10. Do not put your name on this form.

Rank	Description of the Item
____	To be given more responsibility
____	To receive good wages
____	To participate in decisions concerning my work
____	To have job security
____	To be able to achieve on my job
____	To have good working conditions
____	To be recognized for the work I do
____	To receive tactful discipline
____	To have a feeling I am in on things
____	To have an opportunity for promotion

Consider the following suggestions when you analyze the results of your survey:

1. When analyzing the results, consider the group's total responses, rather than individual responses.

2. Where significant rank order differences appear between your responses and those of your employees, consider these to be differing perceptions.

3. If the employees request a summary, make it up and pass it around for their use.

4. If employees wish to discuss the survey results with you, and time permits, do so. However, avoid committing yourself to promises you cannot keep.

5. Study the results carefully and determine what measures, if any, you can take to satisfy the top three rated items.

6. Don't overlook the bottom three ranked items, as these have significant meanings as well.

7. Don't be overly concerned about the semantics of each item, and how individuals may interpret key words in certain items.

8. Above all, if you choose to discuss the results, avoid disagreements. This would defeat your purpose.

9. Finally, the survey results have meaning only to you and your employees. If you choose to take positive steps to improve group relationships based on these results, keep your actions within the group's parameters.

Inner conflicts

Conflicts take place in three different areas of human behavior: between man and nature, between man and man, and within an individual. It is this third area, internal conflict, that we shall examine next.

Inner conflict may stem from several sources. Some managers set unrealistic standards for themselves and thus can never perform to their own satisfaction. Some are afraid of failure, and in trying to arrive at a successful course of action may procrastinate or make unwise, precipitate decisions. Still others are so concerned with what is "right" or "good" that they lose sight of what is best for the organization and for themselves. All these situations set up conflicts.

It is important to be able to resolve these conflicts, to make decisions, to act on them, and if they fail, to learn from them. What you learn from your past failures will make you more successful in the future.

Let's examine some techniques that are aimed at resolving the third type—internal conflicts.

KNOWING WHO YOU ARE—
THE LOOKING-GLASS-SELF TECHNIQUE

One of the best ways we can know who we really are is through the use of the "looking-glass-self" concept. This term was coined in 1902 by Charles Horton Cooley, an American sociologist.*

> The social reference takes the form of a somewhat definite imagination of how one's self . . . appears in a particular mind, and the kind of self-feeling one has is determined by the attitude toward that which is attributed to that other mind. A social self of this sort might be called the reflected or looking-glass self:
> "Each to each a looking-glass
> Reflects the other that doth pass."

Let's describe this technique in another way. Every day each of us imagines how we appear to other people. This includes the totality of our physical makeup, our actions, and our thoughts as expressed through our communicative processes. Then we imagine what the other person imagines, or thinks, about us. How others—subordinates, peer group members, and superiors—act and react to us helps us form an opinion of who we are and shapes our self-identity.

Managers must be careful not to deceive themselves in either of those steps. A manager's role entails such socially recognized and acceptable characteristics as power, authority, and responsibility. How do you imagine or picture yourself exercising power, authority, and responsibility with your subordinates? Furthermore, how do you imagine what others (subordinates, peer group members, and superiors) think about the manner in which you exercise these qualities? Misinterpretation of these two vital steps in the looking-glass-self technique when trying to discover who you are has led many managers astray. This misinterpretation on a manager's part leads into a

*Charles H. Cooley, *Human Nature and the Social Order* (New York: Charles Scribner's Sons, 1902), pp. 183–184.

closely allied second technique that, if studied carefully, can help you.

MAINTAINING CONSISTENCY IN ONE'S RESPONSES TO OTHERS

A firm sense of identity is often reflected and measured by how consistent managers are in their behavior. Inconsistency with subordinates, peer group members, and especially superiors is both confusing and damaging. It causes disagreements and conflicts between managers and subordinates, and far worse, creates an obstacle to one who is trying to establish a sense of self-identity. Thus, inconsistency can be a measure or expression of the internal conflicts the manager is experiencing.

I have known managers who were out-and-out bastards in their work relationships with others. They certainly were not the most popular managers in the organization, but their behavior was consistent and predictable. I've also known managers who were mild-mannered, easygoing individuals. Again, it was easy to predict their behavior. But the manager who fluctuated between these two extremes was the most difficult individual to work with, because his unpredictability kept me off-balance. This poor devil had an array of internal conflicts that were insurmountable.

UTILIZING YOUR FREE TIME MORE EFFECTIVELY

Many managers participate in community activities and social groups and organizations for diversion, out of a sense of civic duty, or to bolster their egos. If you don't overcommit yourself to activities, they can broaden your perceptions and sharpen your leadership skills.

Engaging in several nonrelated outside activities can be draining, however. Furthermore, taking on outside activities that directly interfere with your vocation creates additional conflicts both at work and at home. Ask yourself these questions:

Is it worth being a pillar of strength in the community at the expense of home life or efficiency on the job?

Is it worth winning the title of "Man or Woman of the Year" and losing a promotion, or even your job?

Is it worth making your avocation your vocation, and your vocation your avocation?

Finally, is overcommitment to outside activities worth the additional mental, physical, and emotional strain to your body and mind?

It is important to learn to say no—to become more discriminating in the expenditure of your free time and to limit social activities that drain emotional energy and prohibit you from doing your best as a manager. Your family, your job, and yourself should be the top priorities throughout your work career. The manager who can say no to overcommitment in outside activities is much stronger than the one who may subconsciously use these activities to escape inner conflicts.

LEARNING TO REASON WITH YOURSELF

To resolve inner conflicts, you must develop the ability to reason with yourself. To do this, you must practice how to conduct internal conversations with yourself in private. Simply ask yourself one objective question at a time. Reason through the possible answers by talking back to yourself. If need be, write the question and all the possible answers on a piece of paper.

Examine the question carefully to determine its objectivity, fairness, and application to the problem. Obviously, if you ask yourself an irrelevant question, chances are your answers will be irrelevant. Next, examine each answer you give yourself in an objective manner. Eliminate answers that cannot be considered as solutions to the problem. Assign priorities to the answers, so that you have backup solutions if the first solution is not feasible. Many successful managers have revealed to me in private discussions that they constantly use this self-imposed question-and-answer method to resolve inner conflicts. Some managers can create mental pictures to go along with their internal conversations. These pictures may range from people's faces and gestures to plant layouts, intricate details of machinery or equipment, or geographical locations.

I often ask myself a question out loud so that I can clearly hear that question. Speaking out loud and listening to my own response tends to reinforce this entire technique.

Occasionally, while driving, I have pulled off the road to write down a question and its possible answers, because the internal dialogue was so good that I did not want to lose it. If nothing else, this technique has brought me temporary relief by removing the intensity and anxiety of grappling with my own inner conflicts. This technique is not guaranteed to permanently resolve all inner conflicts, but the answers captured at these moments can lead to more viable solutions.

I believe this technique of internal conversations and self-created dialogues is healthful. The technique relieves tensions and anxieties to some degree, which is much better than keeping them locked inside. Failure to vent inner conflicts can lead to ulcers, hypertension, or a nervous breakdown.

Making conflict work for you

Listed below are some brief guidelines managers should consider when attempting to make conflict work in their favor.

1. Conflict between people is inevitable, but the manner in which it is handled by a manager can be an asset.

2. Conflict once resolved can create innovations, new procedures, and different methods for obtaining mutually acceptable work goals.

3. Conflict, if handled properly by management, can contribute to a deeper and more personal understanding of others' perceptions and opinions. This is especially significant between managers and their superiors, peer group members, and subordinates.

4. Conflict resolution can lessen employee turnover and increase morale and production. It is necessary, however, to establish fair and equitable procedures for resolving conflicts.

5. Conflict is unhealthy when it becomes personal and involves individual personalities. Personality conflicts can leave individuals permanently and socially scarred.

6. People are emotional, and conflict is one means of expressing one's emotions. The most successful managers are those who are able to establish a consistent climate of conflict acceptance and understanding which permits emotional expressions without fear of ridicule or unnecessary punitive discipline.

7. When conflict arises, an effective manager acts quickly to inter-

vene in order to work toward constructive solutions between two conflicting parties.

8. Finally, managers must recognize that not all conflicts are soluble. Some conflicts, despite your best efforts to resolve them, may remain long after their initiation. Therefore, the most practical technique is to learn to live with it. If time is on your side, and quite frequently it is, look for ways to modify the conflict or problem so that you manage it, rather than letting it manage you. Keep in mind that if life were truly a "bed of roses," and conflict did not exist, many of us would be unemployed, or hold totally different jobs from the ones we have. This, in a sense, is the irony of conflict.

CONFLICT CHECKLISTS

The following two checklists are based on the various techniques presented in this chapter. The first checklist is a self-examination of the successful techniques you can use when attempting to resolve conflicts between yourself and others. The second checklist concerns successful techniques to use when resolving inner conflicts.

RESOLVING CONFLICTS BETWEEN YOURSELF AND OTHERS

	Always	Sometimes	Never
1. If you sense an impending conflict is developing between you and another individual, do you attempt to obtain mutual perception of the problem?	——	——	——
2. Do you practice the leveling technique, that is, telling it like it is, with your subordinates?	——	——	——
3. Do you adjust your perception filters when dealing with subordinates?	——	——	——
4. Do you encourage your subordinates to adjust their perception filters when dealing with a problem that concerns you?	——	——	——

	Always	Sometimes	Never

5. Do you believe that using a technique that brings out perceptual differences, or differences of opinion between you and your employees, can resolve disagreements and/or conflicts?

6. If you project your managerial needs upon your subordinates' needs, do you believe this can create conflicts?

7. If you used the survey technique in this chapter and found significant differences between your responses and your subordinates' responses, would you attempt to change those things that are within your authority?

8. When conflicts arise between you and others, do you keep personalities out of it?

9. Do you feel that conflict is one way for people to express their emotions?

10. Do you believe it is possible to make conflict work for you?

RESOLVING INNER CONFLICTS

	Always	Sometimes	Never

1. Do you believe that inner conflict results when an individual compares different interests and courses of action and anticipates their results?

2. Have you ever been afraid of failing?

3. Do you procrastinate?

4. Do you feel that your self-determined standards of performance are realistic?

	Always	Sometimes	Never
5. All of us have experienced failure in the past. Do you think it is possible to learn from your past mistakes?	—	—	—
6. Do you feel that the looking-glass-self technique is a valuable method to use in order to know who you are?	—	—	—
7. Do you as a manager have a sense of your own identity?	—	—	—
8. Do you feel that you behave consistently to others?	—	—	—
9. Do you utilize your own time effectively?	—	—	—
10. Are you selective in the number and types of outside activities you engage in?	—	—	—
11. Have you learned to say no to the temptation of overcommitment in outside activities that are not related to your occupation?	—	—	—
12. Do you engage in internal conversations with yourself when resolving inner conflicts?	—	—	—
13. If a conflict cannot be completely solved, are you willing to learn to live with it?	—	—	—
14. Do you feel that the most devastating conflicts are those we harbor within ourselves?	—	—	—

4 DECISION-MAKING

The Measure of a Manager

Decision-making is the true measure of a manager. Let's break this word into its parts and examine them separately. *To decide is to determine or produce a judgment. To make is to bring something into existence.* Therefore, decision-making is to bring into existence a determination or judgment. This chapter will deal more heavily with decision-making techniques than problem-solving techniques.

Because I have worked in various line and staff functions, I can share with you the decision-making differentials in these two broad areas of management. In this chapter, I have included a short section outlining these differences. For those who wish to test their basic decision-making abilities, I have included a short self-scoring quiz. At the end of the chapter, you will find a decision-making research study and questionnaire which I developed, administered, and published a few years ago. Although the results were not necessarily outstanding, the participating managers' reactions to this exercise proved to be typical of contemporary management. Therefore, I suggest that mid-

51

dle managers and executives read this brief survey and study the questionnaire as an additional technique to use in their own managerial growth and development.

Timing as a technique

Timing is the choosing of the moment or occasion for making or announcing a decision or putting it into action. For instance, a manager's timing for making a decision is most important whenever it is expected that a significant change will be made in the work patterns of employees. Consider the following two successful techniques whenever you are attempting to achieve the proper timing in making an important decision.

THE NEW SITUATION TECHNIQUE

It is sometimes advantageous to a manager to wait until a new situation arises before making a decision. For example, as a manager you may want to make some personnel changes, or even terminate the employment of unsatisfactory workers. Assuming these personnel changes or terminations are justifiable, it's more reasonable to make the decision and take the necessary action during a financial downturn. The timing thus provides a protective shield for such action, and if several employees are involved, chances are the decision will be more acceptable by those concerned.

Other situations for using this technique occur when a new manager takes office, because it is generally expected that significant procedural and personnel changes may take place as a result, and during an expansion within a department or unit. The expansion provides the proper timing for making changes in procedures, systems, rules, and regulations.

HEDGING YOUR BETS

In making decisions, successful managers ask themselves what the possible costs or consequences of failure might be as a result of the decision, and then they "hedge their bets" by creating some opportunity to guarantee a relatively high degree of recovery if events do not work out as planned or desired. Many managers frequently use this technique by committing only a minimum of resources (time, expenditures, and employees) and observing the results. Trial runs or sample installations exemplify the decisions of managers who are intelligently hedging their bets.

Reversing as a technique

Sometimes the easiest way to make a decision is to use the technique of reversing or changing the element that is causing the problem. For example, take the case of a professional golfer in a championship tournament. He has just made a beautiful iron shot that landed short of the green. As he walks down the fairway he discovers his ball has rolled into a small paper bag, carelessly discarded by someone in the gallery. If he removes the ball from the bag, it will cost him a penalty stroke. If he hits the ball and the bag, he will lose control over the shot. Suddenly he reaches into his pocket, takes out a book of matches, strikes one, and sets fire to the bag. After the flimsy bag has burned away, he selects his appropriate iron, addresses the ball, swings, and watches the ball land very close to the cup on the green. Normally, most of us would take the penalty stroke by picking up the bag and emptying the ball out of it. But the golfer has simply removed, or changed, the troublesome element.

Here are some basic guidelines and questions to consider when using the reversing technique.

1. Examine each step in the procedure *leading up* to the step causing the problem.
2. Likewise, examine each step *following* the step that is causing the problem.
3. Can I *change* the order of the steps and move the one causing the problem forward or backward?
4. Can I *eliminate* entirely the step that is causing the problem?
5. Is it possible to *reverse* any of the steps before or after the one causing the problem?
6. Is there a more *simplified* way to do the entire operation?

7. Is it possible to *reverse* the entire procedure?

8. Can I *change* the entire procedure around without causing disruption or creating more problems?

9. Finally, if it is possible to reverse this critical step, will it make my overall decision easier?

Assigning numbers to significant factors

Whenever we make important decisions, we have a tendency to weigh various alternatives and pick the one we think is right. If we have several alternatives to consider, it often becomes difficult to keep track of all of them in our minds. Therefore, it is helpful to list these alternatives, or factors, and rate each on a scale of, say, 1 to 5. You can then see at a glance which are the most attractive alternatives.

As an example, let's assume you want to judge two employees for possible promotion. On the top of a piece of paper write the two employees' names side by side. On the left, list all the important criteria for the new position. Next, assign a number from 1 to 5 opposite each criterion and underneath the employee's name. Assume that 1 is the lowest value and 5 the highest value. If you choose an odd-number rating scale you will eliminate tie scores. Table 1 shows an example of this technique.

According to this evaluation, employee Bill Jones receives a higher rating than Bob Smith. By translating words into figures, you

TABLE 1. Rating significant factors: an example.

Job Criteria	Bob Smith	Bill Jones
Leadership	5	4
Communications	3	4
Responsibility	4	5
Experience	4	5
Job Skills	5	4
Follow Through	3	4
Totals	24	26

can more readily compare all these factors at the same time. This short and simple technique can be adapted to almost any decision-making need.

A few words of caution about this technique are needed at this point.

1. If you choose to use this technique, your table must include *all* the important factors. To omit one could be disastrous.

2. Enough factors should be considered so that the numerical ratings produce a significant differential in the total scores.

3. Ratings must be assigned as fairly as possible. If you permit bias or prejudice to enter into the ratings you might as well throw this technique away. There is less probability of bias or prejudice in rating things or situations than in rating people.

4. This technique should never be used as the only or as the final determinant for a decision.

To summarize then, the value of this technique lies in the fact that it translates general terms, words, or facts into figures so that a concise and brief analysis can be made.

The second solution technique

If you subscribe to the idea that there is rarely, if ever, a single objectively correct method of accomplishing a given aim, the process of decision-making becomes simplified. The old adage that says, "there's more than one way to skin a cat," is very appropriate in this business of decision-making.

When I was a line manager years ago, I was asked to serve as a vacation-relief line supervisor, which entailed supervising different jobs, for different vacationing line managers, and on different turns. It also meant working with different groups of employees, who were conditioned to do the same job, using their methods of work to achieve the same purpose. Being somewhat naive at this type of managing, I kept my mouth shut and simply observed the employees performing their jobs. When a simple production decision had to be made, I turned the responsibility back to the hourly employees, unless, of course, it was a major decision, or an emergency. This experience showed that many different decisions can be used to obtain the same results, and that one decision is often just as applicable as another. There is no one "correct" method of accomplishing a work objective. There may be many correct methods, based on many good decisions that managers can use to obtain their objectives.

Striving for the so-called correct way, for perfection, creates a self-imposed pressure, which prevents many managers from searching for a second and equally acceptable solution. When managers seek a second solution to a problem, they soon discover that originality and creativity become more prevalent in the decision-making process. They also discover that many more effective decisions are forthcoming when perfectionism is set aside, and that originality and creativity are encouraged through the use of second solution techniques.

Learning how to become decisive

Becoming decisive and being decisive are standard qualifications of a successful manager. Below are some guidelines for learning how to become more decisive.

Establish time parameters. There are times you must make snap decisions, and other times when more thoughtful decision-making is necessary. Set reasonable time limits and stick to them.

Define the problem properly before looking for answers. Successful managers know that the trick in effective decision-making is not to find the right answer, but to find the right question.

Spread out a decision. Spread out a decision from beginning to end. Weigh the facts and evaluate the options. Sometimes, less fact-finding and more fact-facing can bring about a quicker and more effective decision.

Don't collect opinions from too many people. Opinions are wonderful in the classroom, but facts substantiate the real world of decision-making.

Distinguish between important and unimportant decisions. Tackle the tough, important decisions head-on, and delegate the lesser decisions to others. Soon you'll find the tough decisions aren't so tough after all.

Don't anticipate every eventuality. Why waste your time with the ifs, ands, buts, howevers, and maybes. Remember, your job is to manage, not crystal-gaze.

Compromise. Don't try to eat your cake and hold on to it. Settle for a roll and a cup of coffee, and you'll find you can make more and better decisions in the long run.

Keep cool. Above all keep calm. When your adrenalin flows excessively, your ability to judge decreases.

Have courage. When everyone is dashing off in different directions, the person who has courage to stand still is probably making the most progress.

Once you make a decision, forget it. Why lose sleep over a decision? There are plenty of "Monday morning quarterbacks" who will give you their opinion, but these people never make the varsity.

Look upon decision-making as fun, not work. Don't take yourself too seriously in this game of life, because you're not going to get out of it alive anyway. Make decision-making fun, not a terrifying chore.

Before and after techniques of decision-making

In the decision-making process both the consequences of a decision and its prelude must be taken into account before an important decision can be made. Therefore, one of the weakest links in the decision-making process is planning the means, methods, and procedures through which the decision is to be put into effect.

Successful managers usually have a comprehensive understanding of both the positive and negative aspects of a decision before they actually make the decision. The skill with which a manager anticipates and avoids the negative aspects of a decision will do much to assure its effectiveness. Therefore, let's discuss the skills and techniques needed prior to making a decision, and the techniques needed to get the desired actions after the decision is made.

Probably the best way to present this line of reasoning is to illustrate the before and after techniques through a series of questions.

THE BEFORE-THE-DECISION QUESTIONING TECHNIQUE

1. How important is this problem to me?
2. How important is this problem to others?

3. How important is this problem to the organization?
4. When should the decision be made?
5. How much of a priority does this problem have over others?
6. When would be the best time to make this decision?
7. If the decision directly involves my employees, what would be the best psychological time to make it?
8. What is involved in terms of costs, materials, and time?
9. What other alternatives or options are available in terms of costs, materials, and time?
10. Who will be directly affected by this decision?
11. Should I consult with others before I make the decision? If so, whom?
12. Have we ever had a similar problem like this in the past? If so, how was it handled?
13. Is this decision going to break away from tradition and routine? If so, will I have the courage to make it?
14. What new problems will be created as a result of this decision? What new decisions can I expect to face as a result of this decision?
15. Is there an expert available within my organization, or outside the organization, with whom I can check on specific facts?
16. To what degree am I being emotional or prejudicial when making this decision?
17. If this is a difficult decision for me to make, why is it so difficult?
18. Should I discuss this decision with my subordinates? Other peer group managers? What will I accomplish by discussing it with others, other than my superior?
19. Have I thoroughly examined every possible option open to me? Have I been fair in weighing other alternatives?
20. Is this decision really going to accomplish what I want it to?
21. If by chance this decision proves to be wrong, what will it cost me? My employees? The organization?

Let's assume at this point in the discussion that you've made up your mind to make the decision. Keep in mind, you haven't changed anything yet. After you make the decision, you must face the consequences of the decision. To help you develop the skills of anticipating the results, you should review the following questions.

THE AFTER-THE-DECISION QUESTIONING TECHNIQUE

1. Who will be responsible for executing each facet and ramification of the decision?
2. How can I measure the effectiveness of the decision? What objective means should I use: Reduced man-hours? Cost reduction methods? Increased productivity? Additional grievances?
3. Am I willing to make concessions shortly after the decision is announced?
4. Will I have to make concessions?
5. Should I develop a schedule to chart each subsidiary goal?
6. Will the required action be plotted in sequential steps?
7. How can I maintain a balance between the inputs and outputs, so that neither can contribute less than is required or more than is needed?
8. What steps must be taken to obtain maximum utilization of all the resources involved?
9. Have I allowed sufficient lead time for procuring materials, supplies, and machinery?
10. Who will be responsible for monitoring and coordinating each important step until the project is completed?
11. What contingency plans must be built into the overall control aspects once the program is under way?
12. How will minor revisions be handled?
13. What communication methods would be best to use once the project has started: Review panels? Group meetings? Posting progress reports?
14. Have I made plans for incorporating flexibility into the program? If so, what are they, and how soon could I put them into operation, if I had to?
15. What warning signals have I built into the system to alert me that the project is falling behind schedule, or getting off target?
16. Is the project equipped to handle emergency decisions?

These are only some of the questions to consider in relation to the consequences of making an important decision.

Finally, remember this: any idiot can make a decision. By this I mean, anyone can say, "Yes, we'll go ahead," or "No, we better hold up," or "Let's wait and see." But it's the successful manager who recognizes that a problem exists, has the courage to make a decision to correct the problem, and has sufficient foresight to be aware of the consequences of his or her decision.

Line and staff decision-making practices compared

There are many managers involved in organizational decision-making processes, but the literature on the subject rarely deals with line managers' decision-making practices. I would like to point out here how line and staff managers differ in these practices.

In order to gain a firm understanding of the two managerial types, consider line managers as blue collar managers, directly involved with production and manufacturing. Staff managers, or white collar managers, are not directly involved with day-to-day front-line production activities. Having served in both line and staff managerial capacities, and in different levels, I can assure you there are vast differences in the decision-making process. Some of these are discussed below.

Line managers rarely have an abundance of time for making a decision, and in any given period of time line managers make far more decisions than staff managers. Many of the decisions made by line managers are routine and repetitive. However, fast action and several decisions are required when emergencies arise. This is seldom true in the case of staff decisions.

Confronted with more face-to-face employee problems than their counterparts, line managers make decisions that are more limited in scope and effect, but just as important. For instance, a staff decision, which might take months to develop, may change the entire operating procedures of a plant and result in widespread changes and ramifications to lower-level line managers and employees. Yet, a bad decision made quickly by a line supervisor can be extremely costly to a plant or department.

A decision made by a line manager cannot be changed, reversed, or erased as easily as one made by a staff manager, and when a line manager makes a bad decision the evidence cannot be hidden, politicked, or verbalized away as easily as a bad decision made by a staff manager. Because their decisions are so much more exposed, line managers probably engage in a greater proportion of risk-taking decisions than staff managers.

Line managers' decisions deal with the day-to-day problems of employees, machines, materials, tools, and the costs necessary for production, whereas staff managers' decisions are geared for ideal conditions. Line managers can experiment only when they are forced to, as a result of a breakdown or changes in the production schedule, or when circumstances are beyond their control. Staff managers, on the other hand, can experiment on paper with several ideas or plans before they make a decision.

Line managers usually execute the decision almost immediately after it is made. This is not necessarily the case with staff managers.

A DECISION-MAKING QUIZ

Decision-making is never an easy, routine job, yet it doesn't have to involve mental anguish. Below are 20 questions with Yes or No answers. Take this simple test and see how you score. The correct answers and ratings are at the end of the quiz.

	Yes	No
1. I can distinguish between big and little problems when making decisions at work.	—	—
2. I normally spend more time on bigger problems, and less time on smaller problems.	—	—
3. I seldom consult and check with anyone when making a decision, because this is a sign of weakness on my part.	—	—
4. I try to avoid crisis decisions.	—	—
5. I try to anticipate all eventualities.	—	—
6. I enjoy running about putting out "brush fires," as this is a mark of an effective manager.	—	—
7. I usually rely on organizational policy to settle routine problems.	—	—

	Yes	No
8. I delegate all my smaller decisions to others.	___	___
9. I am not afraid of failure in my decision-making practices.	___	___
10. I do not put off making decisions.	___	___
11. When making a decision, I concentrate on the problems at hand and exclude other things from my mind.	___	___
12. I don't try to anticipate all eventualities of my decisions.	___	___
13. At times I consult and check with others because it is a sign of strength not to know all the answers.	___	___
14. I always try to have an alternative solution in case my original solution doesn't work.	___	___
15. Many times I make decisions under pressure.	___	___
16. I try to develop decisiveness, because indecision creates tension.	___	___
17. Once I make a decision I forget about it.	___	___
18. I try to avoid making decisions under pressure.	___	___
19. When making decisions I don't expect to be right all the time.	___	___
20. I think the toughest decisions to make are those that concern my employees.	___	___

CORRECT ANSWERS

1. Yes	5. No	9. Yes	13. Yes	17. Yes
2. Yes	6. No	10. Yes	14. Yes	18. Yes
3. No	7. Yes	11. Yes	15. No	19. Yes
4. Yes	8. Yes	12. Yes	16. Yes	20. Yes

Evaluation. Give yourself 5 points for each correct answer. A perfect score would be 100. If you scored the following, rate yourself accordingly:

> 100–90   You should be promoted immediately.
>
> 85–75   You're on the right track, but keep trying.
>
> 70–50   Better not tell anyone, and you probably won't.
>
> 45–25   Are you sure you're in the right job?

25–0   Better see your personnel manager about an
early retirement.

Techniques for processing information

One of the difficulties managers face in decision-making is failure to make full use of the available information. How is it possible for a manager to have all of the information and not use it? Part of the answer seems to be that the brain has a great capacity for storing information but a lesser capacity for processing or recalling this information when needed. Let's discuss some short techniques that are designed to help you process the available information at your disposal.

Look for patterns. When you are reviewing all the available information, some kind of a pattern or relationship should emerge. If it doesn't, then you have probably collected too much irrelevant information, or else there are many decisions to be made, rather than one major decision. For instance, when assessing or evaluating candidates for various positions, I always look for performance patterns that indicate a strong track record in success and upward mobility. Decisions concerning promotions and hiring are much easier if you know what to look for and seek patterns of behavior that are consistent with success.

Guard against complacency. By critically evaluating your approaches to a decision, you can guard against complacency. If, as a manager, you continually emphasize only what you consider to be your strong points and ignore the suggestions of others, you will never make full use of all the available information. Many times, suggestions by others will increase your knowledge and unearth valuable data.

Examine time and space aspects. All decisions contain some element or degree of time. Space aspects, however, may or may not be a primary influence. When processing available information in relation to a decision, try to rearrange both time and space aspects to determine if these elements of information were inadvertently concealed, overlooked, or forgotten.

Avoid jumping to conclusions. Jumping from partial information to what you think is a conclusion or possible solution could very well steer you in the wrong direction and waste a lot of valuable time in your decision-making practices.

If you're stuck on a decision, take a break. Assuming you have sufficient time, and you're really hung up on what decision to make, it might be wise to take a break and get away from it for awhile. Moreover, if you have searched and processed all the available information and cannot reach a decision, then you deserve a break. But if you haven't processed all the information, or given the decision sufficient thought, the so-called break may be nothing more than an evasive move on your part. Too many of these breaks can lead you into procrastination.

Creativity as a technique

Which manager has the best chance to succeed—one who emphasizes conformity to rigid standards and rules, or one who encourages creativity? While creativity may get the nod, all too often conformity is the practice.

What can managers do to develop more creativity in their decision-making practices? Here are some basic techniques that successful managers have learned to use.

Ignore ridicule. Creative managers should be able to express their ideas without enduring derision from others. Where this is not the case, seek help and guidance from your superiors. Creative managers are not afraid of failure or of being laughed at. What is most important to a manager is what the manager thinks of himself or herself. If ridicule persists, or you get no support from your superior, perhaps you should seek employment with an organization that encourages originality and creativity.

Take risks. Managers develop new approaches to problems and try out different decisions only if the rewards for being right are greater than the penalties for being wrong. You never know what the penalties are until you take the risk to find out. When taking risks, start with small decisions first. If they succeed, continue to build your career and reputation slowly and on a well-planned basis. If these first attempts fail, retreat and regroup your strategy, thinking and planning before starting again. In either case, always be prepared to defend yourself and your actions.

Get or give assistance. There's no use acquiring or developing talented managers only to expect them to do routine, menial work. Managers should seek help and encouragement from their superiors in their decision-making roles. And likewise, managers must give help and assistance to subordinates in their approaches to the decisions they are expected to make.

Remove red tape. Rule books breed few ideas and red tape stifles others. Most successful managers, however, aren't afraid to break the rules or circumvent policy whenever warranted. But today, too many managers are willing to take the path of least resistance. Thus they become prisoners of the organization's rules, regulations, and red tape.

Keep yourself well informed. Successful managers keep abreast of new knowledge, are well read, and are familiar with the state of the art in their areas of expertise. By attending seminars, joining professional organizations, and freely discussing ideas with others, both within and outside their organizations, the creative manager is in a better position to make constructive decisions.

Make use of your life experiences. While formal education probably helped get you into your present managerial position, imagination, open-mindedness, and life experiences are your assets now. When managers neglect these latter aspects, they tend to produce discomfort and uneasiness in themselves, and strangle their own creativity.

Be willing to work. A creative manager works harder, concentrates on the problems at hand, and is more dedicated than one who is not creative. This does not necessarily mean long hours on the job, but rather a persistence and determination to keep working on a solution to a problem. I've seen a lot of managers spend 12 to 14 hours per day and accomplish less than others who worked 8 or 9 hours per day. The difference was simply that the former were spending their time unwisely, while the latter worked at solving problems.

At one time in my career I was in charge of a steel plant's methods improvement program. The most outstanding contributor and creative individual was a general foreman of maintenance. In one year he contributed more than 200 substantial money-saving ideas. One day I asked him how he went about developing so many ideas. He looked at me for a moment and said, "If I told you, you wouldn't believe me." I assured him that I would believe him, if he told me his secret. He laughed, looked up in the air, and said, "A lot of my ideas come to me when I'm in the bathroom." I couldn't decide whether he was telling me the truth or was pulling my leg. Apparently my facial expressions gave my thoughts away. I started to open my mouth to speak, when he interrupted me and said, "Believe me, Paul, that's the honest-to-God's truth. In fact," he continued, "I have a pencil and pad in the bathroom, and write down several ideas while sitting there!" I just shook my head. He continued, "You see, at work I am too busy to write these ideas down, but I keep them in my head, and when I get the opportunity at home, and I am relaxed, then I write them down." The point of this story is that the creative manager is constantly working or thinking about solutions to problems and the decisions that must be made.

How to increase your mental powers

Listed below are three short techniques that will multiply your mental powers. You can teach yourself to be a better thinker by practicing these techniques.

Concentrate on what's useful to you. Develop a mental filing system by selective concentration on those things that are useful to you. Teach yourself to filter out those things that are of no interest or value to you, and retain those things that are necessary to your success. In executive board meetings, for example, about 90 percent of the material discussed is totally useless. It's the other 10 percent that you should retain for future reference and action, especially if you are responsible for making certain decisions between now and the next meeting.

Know what's happening to you. By concentrating on the people around you, you can learn a lot about your employees, peer group members, and superiors that you never noticed before. The following anecdote illustrates this technique.

I once sat through several arbitration cases (on the management side of the table) and noticed the president of the local union making notes at inappropriate times. When I asked him about this after the meeting was over, he told me, after some prodding, that when he hears a big word he doesn't understand, he jots it down. Realizing that he was trying to improve a very limited vocabulary, I gave him a book on how to increase one's vocabulary, and told him to study it faithfully. Over the next 12 months the number of arbitration cases decreased, and our friendship increased. Don't misunderstand me. I am not saying that because I helped him with a very personal problem the number of arbitration cases decreased significantly. But we tended to get along much better than before. The fact that I was aware of what was happening around me was a big influence in our relationship.

Learn to classify and relate information. Train yourself to group facts and information together, so that you can reach conclusions much easier. For instance, every time you gain new knowledge that is or will be helpful to you, classify it through association with something similar. If necessary, jot down pertinent information as a means of reinforcement and recall.

One of the very best salesmen I ever met used this technique to a high degree of proficiency. On his first visit to a new client, he would gain as much information about the president of the company as was possible. He would endlessly interrogate the president's secretary, jotting down all kinds of information about the company and the president's personal life. During the initial interview in his discussion with the president he would use part of this newly learned information, and upon leaving would immediately write down additional information. Prior to every follow-up sales call he would religiously review his notes. He soon found that he no longer needed the notes and could recall all this information at a moment's notice. He simply learned to classify and relate pertinent information for each client by using this technique. The payoff, however, came when the client expressed interest in buying his products, and would ask the salesman about certain decisions that had to be made in relation to costs, shipments, quality, and the like. Again the classification technique would be put into practice by the salesman in an effort to finalize the sale.

Decision-making practices

In 1971, while serving as the Training Manager at the Airco Speer Carbon and Graphite Company, in St. Marys, Pennsylvania, I designed and conducted a research program on decision-making practices.* A combined group of 18 middle managers and plant superintendents participated in an evaluation of their plant manager's problem-solving and decision-making patterns. This group included the following personnel: two general production superintendents, two cost managers, two control managers, two industrial engineer managers, two quality control managers, two maintenance superintendents, and six production superintendents. In addition, two individual plant managers were evaluated by their subordinate middle managers.

The questionnaire contained 50 questions grouped in three categories:

1. How does a plant manager make decisions?
2. How shall a plant manager govern his immediate subordinates?
3. How shall an administrator govern an enterprise?

CONCLUSIONS FROM CATEGORY 1

1. Plant managers display several types of decision-making behavior patterns, classified as impulsive, as requiring deliberation and consideration, and as direct delegative decisions.

2. Middle managers consider personnel decision (the people problems) the hardest to make.

3. Middle managers reported they make 83 percent of their own decisions, of which 28 percent are considered by the middle managers to be of major consequence, and 72 percent represent minor decisions.

4. Middle managers claim to have less say or involvement in important decisions concerning their sphere of influence and span of control.

* Paul W. Cummings, "Decision-Making Practices," *Applied Training*, May 1975, pp. 5–18.

CONCLUSIONS FROM CATEGORY 2

1. The two plant managers in this study were very cooperative in assisting their subordinate managers in making decisions about the work organization.

2. Where differences of opinion were involved, the plant managers were able to substantiate their preference for one alternative over another.

3. Middle managers maintained that they would prefer to be responsible for their own decision-making activities.

CONCLUSIONS FROM CATEGORY 3

1. Middle managers felt the toughest decisions facing their plant managers were those concerning personnel. In the private review and discussions with the plant managers this fact was confirmed.

2. A great percentage of the middle managers did not feel the work organization had enough company policy at the time of this survey.

3. Most of the middle managers felt that their plant managers encouraged creative thinking on new approaches and practices in the work organization.

4. All the middle managers were very affirmative in their decision-monitoring systems (or feedback) as well as plant tours and physical inventory inspections in order to determine that decisions were being carried out.

A PERSONAL COMMENT

Throughout the course of this study I frequently had the feeling I was being taken. This entire research study was so new and innovative to these 20 individuals that I personally questioned the credibility of some of the responses given. Middle managers are not only intelligent in the skills required to do their jobs, but are exceedingly aware of the social skills needed to maintain their positions within the organization.

To be given the opportunity to appraise and evaluate one's boss may be an experience thousands of managers have never received, and yet when presented with that opportunity they are extremely careful to avoid making responses which might bring about future re-taliations in one form or another.

The purpose of presenting this brief research on decision-making practices is to encourage the reader to consider using parts or all of the questionnaire as a technique to measure your subordinate's reactions and feelings toward your effectiveness in this broad area of decision-making.

The questionnaire follows. Remember, there are no "right" or "wrong" answers to this survey. Only you, the manager, can interpret the various answers given by your subordinates. If you use this survey with your subordinates, it could be one of the most enlightening experiences in your entire managerial work career.

SURVEY OF DECISION-MAKING PRACTICES

	Yes	No
1. Does your superior frequently make spur-of-the-moment decisions?	___	___
2. Does your superior attempt to weigh various alternative actions prior to making the final decision?	___	___
3. Does your superior seem to take longer to make a decision for you as compared to others with a similar rank to yours?	___	___
4. Are there times when you feel your superior has some unknown reason for not giving you a decision?	___	___
5. Are decisions from your superior usually thorough in detail and/or description?	___	___
6. Has your superior ever given you decisions which you thought were "sketchy" or "fuzzy" in detail or description?	___	___
7. Does your superior seem to take longer than you feel he should to make a decision?	___	___

8. Do you feel you receive a responsive decision (some degree of sensitivity for the situation) when you ask your superior for one?

___Always   ___Usually   ___Never

Yes No

9. Do you feel your superior gives you a clear-cut decision?
__Always   __Usually   __Never

10. Do you feel your superior is vague or hazy in giving you decisions?
__Always   __Usually   __Never

11. Has your superior ever "pulled rank" and by virtue of his vested authority demanded that you follow his orders in solving a problem?   — —

12. If there are differences of opinion between you and your superior as to how to solve a problem, does your superior explain his reasons for selecting one alternative over another?   — —

13. Has your superior ever given you a decision which proved to be wrong? ("Wrong" should be defined as a situation where the consequences of the decision were detrimental to the company's interests.)   — —

14. Have you ever deliberately failed to follow one of your superior's decisions because you knew, felt, or thought it was a poor decision?   — —

15. Do you sometimes think your superior purposefully avoids making a decision?   — —

16. Would you rather share the decision-making with your superior than be responsible for making the decision yourself?   — —

17. Has your superior ever said to you, "This is your decision. Figure it out for yourself."?   — —

18. When you have a really tough problem to solve and seek the advice of your superior, how frequently is he cooperative?   — —

19. What type of decision do you think your superior considers to be the hardest or toughest to make? A decision about:
__Production   __Personnel   __Scheduling
__Costs   __Planning   __Other (specify)

Yes   No

20. Does your superior put you in the position of making snap decisions?
___Always ___Sometimes ___Never

21. What type of decision do you find is the hardest for you to make?
___Production ___Personnel ___Scheduling
___Costs ___Planning ___Other (specify)

22. In a discussion with your superior about a problem, he decides on a course of action which you know is not the best. After you present the facts and state your opinion, does he change his original position or decision?
___Always ___Sometimes ___Never

23. During a typical month you make hundreds of decisions in your job. Assuming 100% equals the total number of decisions you make, estimate the following:
___A. Percentage made by your superior for you
___B. Percentage you make on your own

24. Of the total percentage of decisions you personally make in a month, what percent do you consider to be:
___A. Major decisions in your sphere of influence and span of control
___B. Minor decisions in your sphere of influence and span of control

25. In the job you now have, do you really enjoy making decisions?   ___ ___

26. If you have a major problem to solve, what method do you use most often in your decision-making process?
___Think About It ___Consult Associates
___Sleep On It ___Consult Superior
___Avoid It, If Possible
___Get Facts, Weigh Them, Make Decision

27. Do you feel your superior wants you to consult him on every decision you make which is outside the normal, routine type?   ___ ___

28. Do you feel your superior encourages you to make the majority of decisions on your own?
___Always ___Sometimes ___Never

Yes No

29. Do you feel you have complete (100%) freedom in making decisions in your job?   — —

30. From time to time do you delay making a decision, hoping the problem will correct itself?   — —

31. If you make a major decision in some phase of your work without your superior's knowledge, do you usually try to communicate your decision and action to him?   — —

32. If you answered YES to Question 31, approximately how soon do you normally try to communicate this decision information to your superior?
___Immediately   ___Within an Hour   ___The Same Day
___Within a Day or Two

33. If you answered YES to Question 31 and the superior is not available for the balance of the day, when do you communicate your action and decision to him?
___Call His Home   ___Tell Another Superior
___Tell Him Tomorrow   ___Tell His Secretary
___Write a Memo or Note

34. Do you feel you have a sufficient number of staff meetings each month with others on your level and with your superior?   — —

35. If you answered NO to Question 34, what would you consider to be a sufficient number of staff meetings each month?   1   2   4   (Circle one answer)

36. When scheduling overtime, are you permitted to schedule overtime yourself?   — —

37. As an aid in helping you make decisions, do you feel there is a sufficient amount of company policies in existence at this time?   — —

38. If you answered NO to Question 37, in what areas do you feel an attempt should be made to develop additional company policies?
___Production ___Personnel ___Scheduling
___Costs ___Planning ___Other (Specify)

Yes   No

39. Do you feel your superior encourages creative thinking and gives you freedom to create new approaches
and put them into practice?
___Always   ___Sometimes   ___Never

40. Do you believe that "every jackpot idea was once a
crackpot idea"?   ___   ___

41. Are there times when it is difficult for you to make a
decision because your emotions are involved?   ___   ___

42. Do you find there are different levels of perception
involved between you and your superior in solving problems? Does he frequently see the problem differently
from the way you do?   ___   ___

43. Do you believe that effective managers do not make
a large number of decisions?   ___   ___

44. Do you think you know when a decision must be
based on principles, and when it should be made on the
merits of the case or situation?   ___   ___

45. Which of these is the most time-consuming for you?
___Making a Decision   ___Implementing a Decision

46. Do you feel every decision has some degree of risk-
taking involved in it?   ___   ___

47. Do you have a built-in feedback system in operation
that allows you to monitor the effectiveness of your decisions and how well they are being carried out?   ___   ___

48. Do you frequently check up on your decisions by
making tours and/or physical inventories to see what is
being done?   ___   ___

49. In the past six months which of the following is most
true of the pace or tempo of your decision-making practices?
___Increased   ___Decreased   ___Remained the Same

50. Are there any constructive comments you would like
to make which would be beneficial to your company's
existing policies or practices in the areas of problem-

solving and decision-making? Please use the space
below to share your ideas.

_____

_____

_____

_____

_____

_____

_____

_____

 **DELEGATION**

A Management Investment

To delegate means to commit various selected powers and functions to subordinates who in turn act as your agent or deputy. Delegation is a managerial skill that must be learned through continual practice, and although it has its difficulties it is highly rewarding.

Delegation is a human investment that can pay handsome dividends to any manager at any level and in any organization. It is a non-materialistic, human behavior investment that brings superior and subordinate closer than any other technique presented in this book.

The philosophy of delegation

Managers must understand, agree with, and practice delegation as an integral part of their work style. Furthermore, managers must comprehend why delegation is desirable and necessary if their organization is to be successful. In a very real sense, delegation must be viewed as functioning within the divisions of labor in the organization. In this instance, divisions of labor denote task differentiation and not job specialization. Therefore, if delegation is to succeed in our contemporary work society, it must be willingly accepted and practiced by managers who, in turn, accept and support the actions taken by subordinates.

Finally, the delegator must also realize that he or she does not surrender or shed authority and responsibility to others. In fact, managers must learn to look upon delegation as a continuous sharing process, one in which the delegator maintains the multifaceted roles of guide, teacher, leader, and investor in human dignity, growth, and development.

Managers must have sound knowledge of their subordinates' capabilities and characteristics before investing delegated authority in them. There are three basic ways to gain knowledge about subordinates' capabilities and characteristics. First, examine their personnel records thoroughly. Although many personnel departments are traditionally delinquent in updating employee records, you can often glean pertinent background information about individuals. Such information as education, marital status, age, previous employment, present residence (urban, suburban, or rural), and family size are good starting points toward understanding why people behave as they do.

Second, when time permits, periodically and privately discuss with your subordinates such topics as their leisure time activities, their likes and dislikes, and their attitudes toward their job, the organization, and work in general. In your discussions, go beyond the conventional and superficial subjects—you may discover that your subordinates are very interesting and informative individuals. May I caution you, however, not to make your discussions appear to be third-degree interrogations or probing investigations. And don't expect to learn everything about a person in the course of a monthly 15-minute visitation with the troops. It takes time to build a pattern of understanding of a person's characteristics. Keep in mind that individuals have a tendency to exaggerate as well as to conceal information about themselves and their nonwork worlds.

Finally, the third and perhaps best method of gaining knowledge about subordinates' productive capabilities is to simply observe them performing their work. This can be done with equal ease in both production arenas and office environments. In this manner you can determine their drive, acceptance of work, resolution of minor work problems, interrelationships with others, and individual initiative. In summary, then, by examining subordinates' personnel records, engaging in regular conversations, and observing work behavior, the manager can assess those who will probably be most responsive to future delegation.

Delegating in a union-oriented work climate might be a bit more complex than delegating work in a nonunion, all-salaried work group. What with job descriptions, seniority, and grievance procedures, you must carefully select individuals for future delegation. Many times I have been told bluntly, "That's not in my job description!" (Obviously, I could have exercised my rank, insisting they do the job, and let them grieve after the task was completed, a tactic I have used on occasion.) But I've always found that there are a few individuals who will accept additional chores without complaining to their union representatives that I was exploiting them. Usually, these are the older, more experienced union-eligible employees with whom I have built up a long-standing rapport and mutual understanding. Delegating to union-eligible employees can be successful, but it requires patience, trial and error, and knowledge of your subordinates' capabilities and characteristics.

Preparing subordinates for delegated roles

Subordinates may fail to do what is expected of them because their manager has not prepared them properly to assume added responsibilities. Consequently, they do not know how to do an advanced job, although they may think they do, and this causes problems between them and their superiors. If delegation is to be successful there must be adequate preparation time for the subordinates. Preparation means training, testing, and assessing the results. Let's examine each of these three techniques separately.

TRAINING SUBORDINATES

One of the weaknesses of management in general is that managers do not consider training an important part of their responsibilities. I have proved this fact countless times when consulting for industry. One of the favorite measuring instruments I use with groups of managers to assess their weaknesses and strengths is Donald L. Kirkpatrick's "Supervisory Inventory on Human Relations."* This inventory contains 80 questions, 13 of which concern principles of learning and training. Inevitably, managers answer most of these 13 questions incorrectly, and upon follow-up discussions, they reveal a complete naiveté about this subject. Furthermore, most managers are unwilling to admit that training is one of their most important functions.

With this in mind, let me briefly introduce you to a very effective and successful training technique, known as JIT, or Job Instruction Training. This technique has four basic steps:

1. Tell the employee.
2. Show the employee.
3. Have the employee tell and show you.
4. Have the employee continue practice and you follow up.

The success of this technique depends upon patience, good communications, encouragement, and praise on the part of the manager. It works, it works well, and it should be a part of all managers' development repertoire. Furthermore, there are countless advantages to using Job Instruction Training.

TESTING SUBORDINATES

Prior to testing a subordinate in a delegated work assignment, the manager and subordinate should establish a firm agreement on the standards of performance expected. These standards should be somewhat general, but should include information concerning the quantity and quality of work expected, time of completion, and how the subordinate's performance will be assessed. If I know what's expected of me, then it's up to me to meet these performance standards. Obviously, if I don't know what's expected of me, then I must guess what level of acceptance and performance standards my manager expects. Consequently, if I am not properly prepared, I'm laboring

---

* Kirkpatrick, "Supervisory Inventory on Human Relations," 4380 Continental Drive, Brookfield, Wisconsin 53005.

under a decided handicap that is unfair to me and my superior as well.

Once employees have been properly prepared, they are ready to be tested under actual working conditions. In this instance managers must show personal interest in their subordinates, be willing to give assistance and support, and share their general knowledge with the subordinate. How the subordinates view the interest shown on the part of their managers depends upon the manager's overall attitude. The manager who acts as a snooper or stands over the subordinate every step of the way will defeat the purpose of the delegation assignment.

It is here that managers face one of the most difficult aspects of delegation: that is, learning to live with different approaches to solving the same problem. As we all know, there are immense variations not only in the quality and quantity of work performed, but in the methods and procedures by which work is done. In too many instances, managers have previously done the same job their subordinates are now doing. Thus managers may become disturbed if things aren't done as well as they did them, or if the exact same methods are not used. Even worse, the subordinate may be doing the same work better than the manager once did, and others in the group are beginning to realize it. To a narrow-minded manager and an aggressive subordinate, this could possibly cause uneasiness to both. Keep in mind that in training and testing subordinates, the intelligent manager is one who can always learn something new about a job. Successful managers are those who readily admit when they learn of a better way to do a job, and praise a subordinate for this type of enlightenment.

A manager should permit the subordinate to make a mistake, assuming, of course, it is not a major mistake. Permitting subordinates to make an error, and letting them find out for themselves, is one of the most useful forms of self-training known. For instance, I can tell you not to touch a hot iron, and you may abide by my warning. But if your curiosity gets the better of you, you'll learn the hard way—but you'll learn. After the completion of the training and testing period, the manager should assess the subordinate's results.

ASSESSING THE SUBORDINATE'S RESULTS

As a manager you should make arrangements for proper and periodic feedback about the delegated work assignment so that you can
check the subordinates' progress and correct, if possible, any major
errors that have occurred through commission or omission. If subordinates have met the performance standards and fulfilled the work
requirements, don't try to improve their efforts at this time. Instead,
praise them for a job well done. If, on the other hand, they have not
met the predetermined requirements, indicate what was neglected or
done inadequately. Chances are, your subordinates will not be off
target by much, since you have built in feedback methods, and by
personal observance and periodic guidance you have directed them
toward the proper goal.

I have found, for instance, that the most productive part of assessment occurs when you as manager discuss with your subordinate the
thinking, decision-making, creativity, and challenges that were
required to complete the assignment. The very fact that one of your
subordinates has experienced these facets of the managerial role, with
all its responsibilities and authority, gives the individual a deep insight into your job. This type of sharing is a very sobering experience
for a nonmanagement member of an organization. But it is also an investment in time, people, and the future of the organization, and if
successful, pays large compounded interest in the future. Delegation
with good training, testing, and an equitable assessment brings people closer together in work groups than any other form of work behavior.

Selecting the right job to delegate

When you assign a new job to a subordinate, he or she will inevitably ask questions. This means that you should be thoroughly familiar with the job. If you have done this particular job several times in
the past, you'll be able to determine by the kinds of questions the
subordinate asks whether or not he or she is qualified to handle the
new assignment. But if the new assignment is foreign to both you
and your subordinate, admit it. Reassure the subordinate that

together you'll both work on the project and as the manager you'll give him or her all the support and resources needed to complete the job. Above all, don't fake your way through the new assignment simply because you're the boss.

How do you go about selecting the right job to delegate? Make a list of all the jobs you presently handle, and check off those you know well. Search out those jobs that occur frequently and are time-consuming. Review in your mind the problems that normally arise, and determine if the subordinate can handle these. Next, determine how much authority is required to accomplish the mission. Are you as willing to assign the needed authority as you are to assign the job? Will personalities clash between your subordinate and others he or she must work with in an effort to complete the job? Will you intercede if conflicts arise? There are countless questions you might ask yourself at this point.

Now you're ready to plan the job. On a sheet of paper write the name of the job, its purpose, and expected results. This should be brief and to the point. Next, write down the major chronological steps necessary to do the job. Write down the names of key people, especially if they're in other departments, plants, or in different geographical locations. Keep personalities out of it. State sources of information or records that are needed to compile the data necessary for the job. If authority is needed, and the subordinate will be miles from you, a short memo of introduction with the authority spelled out would be most helpful.

Now assign the job to your subordinate. Obviously, if this is a major job assignment, you'll want to spend a great deal of time privately reviewing the material you've prepared. If you have an example of what the job looks like when completed, you should review this with the subordinate. You might "dry-run" the project from start to finish with your subordinate, permitting him or her to ask questions at any time. Finally, assure your subordinate that he or she has complete authority and is acting in your behalf, and that you will stand behind any decision or act of authority exercised.

You must demonstrate your trust and faith in your subordinate. Part of this has already been accomplished by the amount and degree of preparation you made and reviewed with your subordinate. Nice words of encouragement, a pat on the back, and a firm handshake are fine examples, but tangible proof in the form of written preparation and review reinforce the subordinate's self-confidence and faith in you. Your investment in time and people will pay off.

CHECKLIST OF DELEGATION SKILLS

Listed below are 20 questions to help you determine your skill at delegating and to give you a kind of perception of whether you are under- or overdelegating in your role as a manager. The correct answers, scoring methods, and ratings are at the end of the checklist.

	Yes	No
1. Once you have delegated, do you keep extremely close tabs on work details to make sure a job or assignment is done right?	——	——
2. Do you feel you must be accountable and responsible for everything and everybody in your department or unit?	——	——
3. Are you a perfectionist about details that do not affect the final outcome of a job?	——	——
4. Do you take work home night after night and still feel swamped by job pressures and minor details?	——	——
5. Once you have delegated a job, do your subordinates interrupt you frequently for help and advice?	——	——
6. Do you feel it's weakness on your part to seek a subordinate's assistance to help you with your work assignments?	——	——
7. After delegating a work assignment, do you get apprehensive about it?	——	——
8. After delegating a work assignment, do you secretly fear that your subordinate may do a better job than you could?	——	——
9. Do you spend a lot of time doing work for your subordinates that you know they could do themselves?	——	——
10. After delegating a work assignment do you secretly fear that your subordinate might do a poor job which would reflect adversely on you?	——	——

Yes No

11. Do you fully realize the potential value of good delegation to a subordinate's development? ___ ___

12. Do you enjoy reserving those easy job assignments for yourself even though you know your subordinates could do them? ___ ___

13. Do you provide all the necessary background information, data, and instructions relative to a delegated job? ___ ___

14. Do you spend as much time on details as you do on planning and managing? ___ ___

15. Do you understand the complete job of delegation and the benefits to be derived from effective delegation? ___ ___

16. Do you believe that a manager should be overworked in order to earn his salary? ___ ___

17. Do you continually postpone work assignments until you get time to do them? ___ ___

18. At the present time are your subordinates prepared to take on more responsibilities? ___ ___

19. Do you train and develop your subordinates to accept increasingly difficult and complex duties and assignments? ___ ___

20. Do you believe that a good manager is one who picks good subordinates to do what he wants done, and exercises self-restraint to keep from meddling with them while they do it? ___ ___

CORRECT ANSWERS

1. No	**6.** No	**11.** Yes	**16.** No
2. No	**7.** No	**12.** No	**17.** No
3. No	**8.** No	**13.** Yes	**18.** Yes
4. No	**9.** No	**14.** No	**19.** Yes
5. No	**10.** No	**15.** Yes	**20.** Yes

Evaluation. Give yourself 5 points for each correct answer. A perfect score would be 100 percent. Rate yourself as follows:

100–90   You're an excellent delegator and deserve a promotion.

85–70   Better check the ones you missed and take corrective action.

65–50   You're not a delegator, you're a confiscator.

45 or less   Good luck in your new job with a different organization.

KNOWING WHEN TO DELEGATE

One of the problems many managers face today is knowing when to delegate. By studying the operations of your department and answering the following questions, you will gain insight and answers to this problem of knowing when to delegate.

1. Does the work slow down or halt when you're away from the job?

2. Do you always seem to be bogged down in details?

3. Do simple jobs in your unit or department seem to take forever to get done?

4. Are unexpected and unwanted emergencies constantly occurring in the area you manage?

5. Do your subordinates always wait for you to give the signal before they begin a job or work assignment?

6. Do you find that the work produced in your group consistently fails to follow your plans?

7. If you were unexpectedly hospitalized for a month or so, could someone in your department carry on in your absence and do a respectable job?

8. If you were offered a big promotion suddenly, but it depended upon a qualified replacement for your job, could you nominate or suggest one of your subordinates?

9. Do you find that you're always pressed for time to get your daily job done, and you have absolutely no time to plan your work into the future?

10. Do you and your superior ever discuss delegating part of your work assignments to your subordinates?

11. Do you delegate work only when you're forced to?

SUGGESTED ANSWERS

1. No	**4.** No	**7.** Yes	**10.** Yes or No
2. No	**5.** No	**8.** Yes	**11.** No
3. No	**6.** No	**9.** No	

I hope for your sake that you answered Yes to questions 7 and 8. However, if you honestly answered Yes to several of the other questions, you had better consider delegating more of your work to your subordinates.

Delegate what you know best

How many times have you said, or heard other people say, "If you want a job done right, do it yourself"? But often managers do not delegate because they do not know how to control the performance of the subordinate, control timetables, or get feedback that will free them from personally participating in an operation. The basic rule for correcting this fear of losing control is simple: Delegate that which you know and love, and assume for yourself that which you dislike but are capable of doing.

By delegating jobs or work assignments that you know best, you can accurately ask the right questions, understand what charts and graphs say, and almost predict the outcome of the assigned job. When you try to control a delegated job which you know little about or do not like, you lack the background and prior experience to anticipate each succeeding step. Furthermore, if your subordinates know that they have been assigned a task you dislike, they may resent you for dumping the undesirable work on them. Managers who shed distasteful work seriously hamper their ability to get ahead in the company because they fail to broaden their knowledge of all the responsibilities inherent in their department. By avoiding new experiences and new knowledge managers inhibit their ability to delegate at a later date.

Why managers don't but should delegate

Listed below in the lefthand column are several reasons why many managers don't delegate work responsibilities to their subordinates. The successful manager's answers to his reluctant counterpart are presented in the righthand column.

The Reluctant Manager	*The Successful Manager*
1. I don't have time to delegate.	1. I take the time to delegate.
2. I want the job done my way.	2. I've found from experience there are many ways to do a job.
3. If I delegate this job and the subordinate messes up, I'll look bad.	3. When I delegate a job to my subordinates, I make sure they don't mess it up.
4. If I delegate this job and my subordinate does as well as I would, he or she will make me look bad.	4. When I delegate a job to my subordinate and he or she does as well as I would, I know it makes me look good.
5. I can do it better myself.	5. I know I can do it better myself, but I want others to know how to do it.
6. I'd rather do it myself than go to all the trouble of telling someone else how to do it.	6. I don't mind training my subordinates; after all there were a lot of people who helped me in the past.
7. If I do it, I know it will get done!	7. If I do it, then I am the only one in the organization that knows how it should be done.
8. I never send a boy out to do a man's job.	8. I don't hire boys in the first place. I hire mature adults and expect them to accept responsibility, and to learn and grow in my department.
9. If I delegate this job to one of my subordinates, I'll have	9. When I delegate a job to subordinates, I want them

The Reluctant Manager	*The Successful Manager*
to check every step he or she does.	to come to me only when they're stuck. I want to develop self-confidence in my subordinates.
10. Delegation is a waste of time.	10. To me, delegation is an investment of time.
11. I'll never delegate my authority to my subordinates. They wouldn't know how to handle it.	11. I'm very selective in delegating my authority to my subordinates—it gives me insight into how they handle various work problems.
12. Delegation? I am all for it, especially those tough jobs I hate to do.	12. I delegate those jobs I know best and tackle the tough ones. In that way, my subordinates and I both learn something new.
13. I don't have enough time to train an assistant.	13. I take time to train my subordinates, because this will provide me with more time in the future.
14. To tell you the truth, my subordinates couldn't handle delegation.	14. I have the utmost confidence in my subordinates. When I train, test, and assess my subordinates, they learn how to handle delegated work.
15. My subordinates would make too many mistakes that I'd have to correct.	15. When my subordinates make a mistake, I want them to learn something from that mistake. After all, I am not perfect myself.
16. Delegate? Are you kidding? I might delegate myself right out of a job!	16. Delegate? You bet I do. If I am sick or absent I want my department to run smoothly without me. Anyway I ex-

The Reluctant Manager   *The Successful Manager*

pect to be promoted soon
and I want a qualified replacement for my present
job.

17. I can do the job myself
    much faster.

17. I've done this job many
    times, but I've got other
    more important things to
    do.

18. Delegate? I've worked too
    hard and too long to get
    where I'm at, and besides I
    must maintain my prestige
    and status.

18. I believe in sharing my so-
    called prestige and status
    through delegation. I want
    my subordinates to experi-
    ence my problems. At any
    rate, I pay my bills with
    cash, not prestige and sta-
    tus.

19. My subordinates are up to
    their ears in work. I can't
    delegate additional work to
    them. They know it and
    that's why I am so popular
    around here.

19. I try to keep my department
    well organized, so that I can
    plan effectively and delegate
    with efficiency. I've been
    told I am well respected by
    my subordinates.

20. To tell the truth, I am just
    not sure how, when, where,
    and what to delegate.

20. There's a certain amount of
    risk in delegation, but I had
    to start somewhere, and
    now I find it's quite easy to
    do.

21. I know my boss would get
    upset if I started to dele-
    gate. You know what I
    mean—gotta keep the boss
    happy.

21. My boss and I discuss my
    delegation strategies. We
    don't always agree, but he's
    never told me to stop. In
    fact, he doesn't mind
    delegating some of his work
    to me.

22. Listen, you can't get these
    younger kids to accept more

22. The young people I hired
    want more responsibility

The Reluctant Manager

responsibility. All they want is more money for less work—it's terrible today.

23. I don't mind experimenting with delegation, but one mistake could be costly.

24. Look, there are just some jobs that I can't delegate— and that's that.

25. I get paid to make the decisions around here, not some flunky!

26. I know what my employees can do and can't do—forget delegation.

The Successful Manager

and become unhappy doing menial tasks. They're rewarded monetarily and have never complained about being overworked and underpaid.

23. I know a mistake would be costly, but I have a built-in control system that eliminates costly mistakes.

24. I made a careful examination and study of my job. By using proper assignments, good controls, performance standards, and assessments, I could delegate any phase of my job to someone in my organization. I hate to say it, but if I dropped dead tomorrow, my department would continue to function and the work would get done.

25. I receive a good salary, but I realize the more exposure I give my subordinates in making decisions the stronger my department becomes, and the better organization we develop.

26. I am not sure what the limits of my employees' capabilities are, that's why I like to "stretch" them once in awhile. Delegation helps me do this.

The Reluctant Manager	The Successful Manager
27. This is a tough union we have here. Once I started delegating, I'd get hit with a thousand grievances.	27. Yeah, it's a tough union— but I know who I can give additional responsibility to, without getting hit with a grievance.
28. Delegate around here? Listen, the big boss promotes people he likes—why bother?	28. I make it a point to tell the big boss who accepts delegation around here. In fact, the big boss promoted three of my people in the last year.
29. I've thought about delegation, but I am too busy, and every night I take work home to get caught up. Even my wife complains.	29. My life outside of this organization is my own. I enjoy my family and social activities. I very seldom take work home, because I practice delegation.
30. Delegate? You bet I do! See good old Joe over there, he's been doing that job for me for the past 10 years— good man, I'd be lost without him.	30. Delegate? I try to. See Joe over there at work? That's the third major job I've given him in the past two months. By this time next year, I want him to know as much as I do about this department.

6 DISCIPLINE

Teach So As to Mold

In countless training sessions I have conducted, I have been amazed to hear managers define discipline almost always in terms of punishment. Yet, according to Webster, it also means "to train by instruction or exercise." Whenever supervisors and managers accept discipline as teaching, molding, instructing, educating, and working with their subordinates, they find that the need for punitive discipline diminishes. Whenever the teaching aspect of discipline is missing, an employee develops a vengeful attitude and tries to get even with his or her superiors. And when only punitive disciplinary methods are used, the employee naturally feels that he or she was treated unfairly and develops a negative attitude. Any manager entrusted with authority and power can punish a subordinate. But the successful manager knows that patiently teaching, training, and instructing subordinates can mold an outstanding work force that needs few, if any, punitive disciplinary measures to accomplish its mission. This chapter illustrates successful techniques of discipline as an educational rather than a punitive force.

A CHECKLIST FOR MEASURING YOUR PREDISCIPLINE MANAGEMENT BEHAVIOR

This checklist presents a series of questions regarding your managerial behavior in relation to the actions you should take to prevent the need for future discipline. It encourages you to examine the full meaning of the word "discipline," and provides guidelines or suggestions that you can use when interacting with your subordinates. The checklist also serves as an introduction to some of the techniques presented in this chapter. This checklist has been designed primarily to help obviate the need for punitive discipline.

	Yes	No
1. Do you know the difference between punitive and nonpunitive discipline?	——	——
2. Do you subscribe to the theory that if a manager follows sound principles and practices, he or she should never have to take punitive disciplinary action?	——	——
3. Have you ever looked up the definition of "discipline" in a dictionary?	——	——
4. Have you ever had the opportunity to attend a group training session in which discipline and the administration of discipline were discussed?	——	——
5. When constructing rules, policies, and procedures in your span of control, do you take into account contemporary customs?	——	——
6. When you've made a new rule, do you make sure that everyone knows it, and are you able to prove that everyone knows it?	——	——
7. When enforcing the rules, do you make exceptions?	——	——
8. Do you believe that by setting a good example, that is, by being well disciplined, you can inspire similar behavior throughout your department?	——	——
9. Do you believe that by establishing a close relationship with subordinates, that is, by showing interest in their work, helping them with problems, and giving recognition, you can reduce the need for discipline?	——	——

                                                                   Yes   No

10. Do you sincerely try to create a friendly atmosphere
within your department and with your subordinates?   ___   ___

11. Do you try to maintain consistently high standards of
performance and give your employees the opportunity to
make satisfying achievements?   ___   ___

12. Do you knowingly permit inferior work to pass unno-
ticed?   ___   ___

13. Do you believe that it is self-discipline that distinguishes the mature manager?   ___   ___

14. Do you believe that self-discipline is measured by
self-control in the face of adverse circumstances?   ___   ___

15. With regard to self-discipline, do you tackle the
tough parts of a job first and get them out of the way?   ___   ___

16. Do you train yourself not to be upset, angry, or hurt
when someone criticizes you?   ___   ___

17. Do you believe that today's young people pose a
special problem for managers?   ___   ___

18. Do you believe that young people, especially those
employed for the first time, should be taught proper on-
the-job behavior as quickly as possible?   ___   ___

19. Do you carefully and fairly review and appraise the
work experience of all new employees during the early
phases of their employment?   ___   ___

20. Do you believe that the best discipline is self-discipline?   ___   ___

21. Do you believe that the foundation of good em-
ployee discipline is good instruction?   ___   ___

22. Do you believe that your subordinates want to know
what is expected of them?   ___   ___

23. Do you think it's possible to develop a work group
whose members will enforce their own group discipline?   ___   ___

24. Do you believe that a manager's problems never
come from discipline itself, but rather from the absence
of it?   ___   ___

Yes   No

25. Do you believe that managers who rely solely on punitive discipline to gain their objectives are putting a
burden on themselves?   ___   ___

26. Do you believe that the real meaning of discipline is
to train, educate, instruct, regulate, correct, and if necessary, to punish?   ___   ___

27. Do you believe that each time you discipline an employee in a punitive manner, you have failed to motivate
him or her as well as you could have?   ___   ___

Answers. All recommended answers should be Yes with the exception of questions 7 and 12.

The early appraisal method

Managers can rarely use the excuse that their failure to accomplish a job or project was the fault of subordinates who failed in
their tasks. The responsibility for getting the job done rests far more
with the manager than with those who are managed. Deficient training or no training, improper conduct, poor work habits, or other
faults of employees should be countered first with an understanding
attempt to have them corrected. This must be done as soon as flaws
are observed. Young people, especially those employed in their first
permanent work position, should be taught proper on-the-job behavior as soon as possible.

Early remedial action on the manager's part reduces the need for
future disciplinary action. Obviously, obtaining good work from ineffective or unwilling subordinates becomes much more difficult if poor
situations are allowed to deteriorate. Therefore, the work performance of all new employees, including novices as well as older, experienced, transferred subordinates, should be carefully observed, reviewed, and appraised during the first 60 to 90 days of employment.

In most organizations, all new employees are given a 60- to 90-day
probationary period. But what does management do during this
period regarding appraisals or evaluations? Very few managers cor-

rect new employees during this period. Most managers patiently wait for the time to pass, then they conduct their probationary period appraisal. Here is where they make their biggest mistake. This is the time to train, instruct, correct, tell, show, and in general encourage new employees to do what is expected of them, not after the probationary period is completed. Now is the time they will make honest mistakes, and if these mistakes are not corrected, the employees naturally assume this is the normal way to do the job. There is no rule or policy that states that a manager is forbidden to correct, evaluate, or appraise new employees' work habits each day during the probationary period.

Some years ago, when I was a labor foreman, all new employees, or new hires, came through my department and were assigned the usual pick-and-shovel jobs. During the first 30 days when assigning work, I would daily indicate to these new recruits that I planned to observe their work behavior. I stressed the fact that I was not looking for gold-brickers, lazy employees, or indifference toward work, but rather wanted to observe their body movements, so that I could help them work more easily, more safely, and with more confidence. I further told them that any corrections or suggestions I made to any individual were to be considered as constructive, rather than destructive or personal. I kept my word each and every day with all my men.

I soon realized that when my subordinates tried the simple little techniques I showed them with a pick and shovel, they found they could accomplish the same job without tiring as fast, were ready to learn more, and realized that I was on their side. By the time their probationary period of 90 days was over and I was required to submit and review a written appraisal on each individual, I could do it with complete honesty and fairness and a sense of accomplishment on both my part and that of my subordinates.

The same technique can and should be applied in any area of work. It requires time, good communications, and a complete and thorough understanding that as a manager you are going to observe an individual do a job from start to finish. Don't hide behind building columns, file cabinets, or desks, but rather stand closely by and watch each move and motion. Correct with understanding and encouragement, and once the job is mastered, indicate to the individual your satisfaction with his or her performance. Remember, there were times in your early work career when you were faced with a new situation or circumstance, and because of lack of experience did not perform like a polished professional.

It is important to refrain from ever reprimanding a new employee in public. You may think you are correcting a bad situation, but all you succeed in doing is humiliating your employee. Moreover, the repercussions of such impulsive disciplinary action are devastating to the department.

Successful preventive discipline techniques

GROUP TRAINING SESSIONS

Large companies or corporations maintain uniform discipline by standardizing the basic rules and conduct and publicizing them both to their employees and supervisors. In addition, they conduct specific training programs for all levels of management. Groups of 15 or so individuals are confronted with typical problems that have been experienced in the past within the organization. These problems range from absenteeism to theft of company property to separation.

Members of the industrial relations or personnel department are present at all sessions, but only to aid in the interpretation of current labor contracts, policies, rules, and regulations. The sessions are led by middle management individuals who have firsthand knowledge and experience in the field. The purpose of these group conferences is to reinforce managers' familiarity with present policy, and to exchange ideas on how to effectively use corrective discipline rather than punitive discipline. The older, more seasoned managers who attend the sessions are encouraged to relate their experiences, so that the younger, less experienced supervisors and managers can benefit from frank and candid discussions. Hypothetical case studies are never used, but only those actual cases that are applicable to the participants and the company. These organizations do not lay down a strict set of rules, but define parameters within which to operate. Finally, a good deal of emphasis is placed on preventive discipline rather than punitive discipline.

CREATING FAVORABLE CONDITIONS

Managers who stress what to do before the fact tend to get better results from their subordinates. They avoid disciplinary problems by creating conditions in which their subordinates are more interested in doing a good job than in not doing the job at all. But how does one create favorable conditions? It starts with managers' attitudes toward their subordinates. By approaching subordinates as human beings who are capable of knowing and using self-discipline, managers create challenging work situations which normal individuals accept and attempt to meet. But it goes further than that.

I have found from past experience that you cannot teach self-discipline to others. They must learn it on their own. And one of the best ways to help subordinates become aware of self-discipline is for the manager to set a good example. Many times a subordinate's work behavior merely reflects that of the superior. If you are a well-disciplined manager, the chances are that most of your subordinates will try to model themselves after you. Not everyone, of course, but many will. On the other hand, if you exhibit a lack of self-discipline, by coming in late, taking excessively long lunch breaks, and demonstrating a generally haphazard attitude toward work, many of your subordinates will emulate your behavior patterns. The old saying "What's good for the goose is good for the gander" is very appropriate in this situation.

Of all the bosses I've reported to, the one I will always remember best was "Bucky" Walters, who was superintendent of a steel-producing mill when I was a young turn foreman. He consistently took a special interest in all his men; he praised in public and reprimanded in private; he would stop what he was doing in order to help anyone; he reported early and stayed late on many occasions; he played no favorites among 50 or so supervisors and middle managers; he would tell you beforehand what he expected from you in the way of performance; he had little use for tattle-tales and apple-polishers, and if you had a problem at work or at home, he was always willing to offer his guidance and counseling abilities—but only if you asked him. I suspect that these are but a few of the qualities that make up a well-disciplined manager, one whom others can model themselves after.

There are other techniques that successful managers can use in this area of preventive discipline. For instance, by establishing a close working relationship with each subordinate, the manager can give verbal recognition to a job well done. When subordinates feel they are ignored, they may not try so hard in the future. When managers solicit help from subordinates rather than giving stern orders, they invite pride, initiative, and productivity to come forward. For example, when a manager brings in subordinates to help solve a problem, uses their suggestions, and includes them in the plans necessary to solve it, then the subordinates have partial ownership in the strategy, and will work doubly hard to make it a success. This is constructive, training discipline.

Self-discipline

Undoubtedly, the most important technique of discipline for a manager to learn is that of self-discipline. We all have likes and dislikes with respect to people, habits, rules, regulations, and our jobs. But self-discipline distinguishes the mature and successful manager from the immature and struggling manager. Self-discipline is the extent to which individuals control their reactions when a circumstance or situation isn't to their liking, and the effort they make to overcome their dislikes.

For instance, learning to accept individuals you dislike and doing jobs you dislike are but two examples of managerial self-discipline. But how does one accomplish this? First, teach yourself not to be hurt or angry when someone criticizes you. Instead of verbally attacking them, refrain from saying something you may regret later on. If the individual is really justified to some degree in criticizing you, then work at forming habits that will be more acceptable. Here are some ways to begin to change:

1. Believe you can break the old habit and form a new, more constructive one.
2. Make sure you sincerely want to change. To do this, you must tell yourself the reason(s) why a different habit is important to you.

3. Determine what the benefits will be to you, if you can successfully change and maintain the new habit.
4. Determine what sacrifices you will have to make in order to achieve your goal. Will the sacrifices be worth the goal you wish to achieve?
5. Attack the change a little at a time and build upon your successes. Each time you act toward achieving your goal, you're one step closer toward that goal.

The supervisory inventory on discipline

Discipline is one of the most complex and least understood functions in contemporary management. Many companies and corporations conduct formal training programs about their current labor contract, its interpretation, and its administration, but few have in-depth programs concerning discipline, per se. While it's true many organizations will teach their supervisors and managers how to administer punitive discipline, the grievance procedure, and the review of past arbitration cases, few attempt to measure a manager's understanding and overall approach to discipline.

Some years ago as a training director, I found an excellent measuring instrument which determines the need for management training in the field of discipline. This instrument, called the "Supervisory Inventory on Discipline,"* is applicable for both union and nonunion organizations, and can be administered to various management groups by any level of management. This inventory measures one's knowledge of discipline and its application, but it is not a test. It contains 80 questions which can be answered in 15 minutes. Its value to managers is that it provides insight into a group's understanding of discipline, the discipline process, and potential problems that can arise because of a fundamental lack of understanding of the subject. The instrument does not conflict with your present labor contract, rules, regulations, policies, or procedures dealing with discipline.

The "Supervisory Inventory on Discipline," or SID, provides a manager with insight about other managers' or supervisors' awareness

* Earl J. Wyman, "Supervisory Inventory on Discipline." Box 200, Delafield, Wisconsin 53018. Copyright 1973.

and understanding of such critical areas in discipline as the causes of discipline problems, communications, disciplinary principles and concepts, penalty-setting processes, rule-enforcement processes, rule-making processes, and taking disciplinary action. Once a manager is armed with this information, he or she can provide additional on-the-job coaching and counseling to subordinates.

This instrument is extremely useful in group conference discussions. When a group of subordinate managers and supervisors have completed the inventory, the individuals score their own inventories and then discuss differences of opinions concerning certain answers. Discussion of different answers and the sharing of opinions causes a cross-fertilization of ideas, which broadens an individual's approach to handling discipline. Admittedly, it is difficult to measure behavior modification of managers and supervisors, but it is agreed that a change in knowledge must take place before an on-the-job behavioral change can occur.

As a successful management technique, SID can effectively reduce the number of grievances and organization experiences. This is because SID develops a team approach to discipline among all first-line blue and white collar supervisors and middle managers. It is vitally important for a common thread to exist in an organization's philosophy, attitude, and administration of discipline.

Reprimanding the prima donna and the outstanding worker

How do you handle the subordinate who's become a prima donna? Having made the judgment that the individual in question is demonstrating prima donna work behavior patterns, you must try to determine what has caused this type of behavior.

I once had an employee who acted like a prima donna because he thought he had a protector in an uncle who was vice president of the organization. In a discussion with him about his behavior, I let him know that I would review his behavior with his uncle. I wanted to make sure that he knew that I expected him to behave in the same manner as the others regardless of his family connections. His uncle completely backed me, and the individual in question stopped showing off, settled down, and became a good worker.

On very rare occasions a manager may have to take steps to reprimand an outstanding worker. Again, it is necessary to determine the reason for such unusual behavior. If the individual thinks he or she is indispensable, is better than you, or can do your job better, I suggest you take time to discuss the problem thoroughly. In this type of a situation a manager could rapidly lose part or all of the control of the group. The point is, never be afraid to lose a good employee if you cannot correct or change the situation. Once you have lost control of the group, out of a fear of losing an outstanding worker, you may end up being the total loser yourself.

The self-inflicted reprimand

A mild reprimand can be subtly administered by asking a subordinate a pertinent question, the answer to which is an automatic self-inflicted reprimand. For instance, let's assume that one of your subordinates has been working for an hour or so on a task that is totally unnecessary, and in essence is a waste of time. Both you and the individual know that this effort is needless. By simply asking the subordinate's opinion of the need to do this worthless task, you avoid humiliating the individual. The success of this technique depends on the form the question takes. It should not be phrased as a direct question like, "What are you doing?" This direct approach on the manager's part suggests an accusation. Immediately the subordinate becomes defensive and tries to protect his or her actions, which defeats the entire technique of a self-inflicting reprimand. By using an indirect question, such as, "How much rechecking do you think safety belts need?" forces a judgmental answer. The question delicately insinuates rather than crudely asserts your disapproval of the subordinate's actions, and in giving his or her opinion the subordinate gets the message.

The sandwich technique

This technique is constantly and skillfully used by many managers when dealing with their subordinates. Basically it consists of a direct verbal reprimand, followed by a mild approval, and concluded with a milder reminder reprimand. In effect, the manager is sandwiching his or her approval in between two reprimands all of which are conducted at the same time.

For instance, a subordinate commits a minor direct violation of a rule in order to get a job done. As a manager you're pleased the job was completed, but you and the subordinate both realize that a degree of risk was taken which could have caused problems. However, had the subordinate attempted to complete the job in the normal fashion it may have taken much longer and created other problems. The manager may say something like this to his or her subordinate: "Joe, don't ever do that again! But now that it's done, I am glad it's completed. But please, don't do it that way again, or we'll both be in trouble." These three statements—a reprimand, an approval, and a reminder reprimand—followed by a slight smile, can be a powerful bond when fortifying the cooperation and loyalty of the subordinate, who otherwise may become alienated by a reprimand alone.

A CHECKLIST TO USE WHEN ADMINISTERING PUNITIVE DISCIPLINE

Since managers do not normally administer punitive discipline every day, there's a natural tendency to forget critical areas that should be reviewed in a disciplinary interview. Therefore, this checklist covers all the important aspects from the start of a disciplinary case to follow-up months later. Please use it as a guideline for each important phase when administering punitive discipline.

You will find some unusual questions in this checklist that have resulted from my own personal experiences in this area of discipline. When you come upon these questions, they should stimulate your thinking and give you insight into areas others have not written about.

____ 1. Have all other measures been exhausted before I administer discipline (training, appraisal discussions, and counseling interviews)?

____ 2. When did the rule violation occur, and have I moved as promptly as possible?

____ 3. Have I secured all the necessary facts, not just opinions?

____ 4. Have I checked the employee's previous record of offenses, or rule violations?

____ **5.** Did I investigate all other sources of information, such as other employees or managers who may know about the case?

____ **6.** Have I verified, if possible, all the facts in the case?

____ **7.** After having checked and verified all the facts, do I know why I want to discipline the employee?

____ **8.** Is it possible to conduct the discipline interview in private so as to avoid embarrassing the employee?

____ **9.** Did I conduct the discipline interview as soon after the offense as possible?

____**10.** Did I permit the employee the opportunity to state his case fully?

____**11.** Did I begin the discipline interview with a question or request for information, rather than an accusation?

____**12.** Did I point out the evidence I have, and then permit the employee to defend himself or herself (point for point, and item for item)?

____**13.** Did I avoid arguing over the facts?

____**14.** Did I keep the discipline interview atmosphere as relaxed as possible?

____**15.** Did I remain cool and calm during the interview?

____**16.** If the employee admitted he or she made an honest mistake, did I take this into consideration later on?

____**17.** If the employee admitted he or she made an honest mistake, did I try to find out why (lack of knowledge, training, or an attitude problem)?

____**18.** Is it possible that other employees could make the same honest mistake, but with more severe consequences (lost time accidents, a fatality, or costly damage to company property)?

____**19.** During the discipline interview did I consistently treat the employee as a mature adult by avoiding scolding tactics?

____**20.** Am I sure that in some way, directly or indirectly, I was not partly to blame for my subordinate's behavior?

____**21.** Are others partly responsible for the subordinate's behavior (playing a trick or joke on the suborindate, or relating bad information to him or her)?

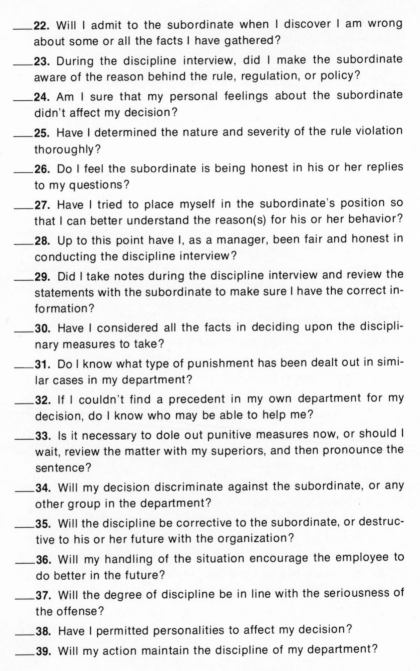

___**22.** Will I admit to the subordinate when I discover I am wrong about some or all the facts I have gathered?

___**23.** During the discipline interview, did I make the subordinate aware of the reason behind the rule, regulation, or policy?

___**24.** Am I sure that my personal feelings about the subordinate didn't affect my decision?

___**25.** Have I determined the nature and severity of the rule violation thoroughly?

___**26.** Do I feel the subordinate is being honest in his or her replies to my questions?

___**27.** Have I tried to place myself in the subordinate's position so that I can better understand the reason(s) for his or her behavior?

___**28.** Up to this point have I, as a manager, been fair and honest in conducting the discipline interview?

___**29.** Did I take notes during the discipline interview and review the statements with the subordinate to make sure I have the correct information?

___**30.** Have I considered all the facts in deciding upon the disciplinary measures to take?

___**31.** Do I know what type of punishment has been dealt out in similar cases in my department?

___**32.** If I couldn't find a precedent in my own department for my decision, do I know who may be able to help me?

___**33.** Is it necessary to dole out punitive measures now, or should I wait, review the matter with my superiors, and then pronounce the sentence?

___**34.** Will my decision discriminate against the subordinate, or any other group in the department?

___**35.** Will the discipline be corrective to the subordinate, or destructive to his or her future with the organization?

___**36.** Will my handling of the situation encourage the employee to do better in the future?

___**37.** Will the degree of discipline be in line with the seriousness of the offense?

___**38.** Have I permitted personalities to affect my decision?

___**39.** Will my action maintain the discipline of my department?

___**40.** Will my actions make me a better manager?

___**41.** Will I learn something from this situation that will be helpful to me in the future?

___**42.** Did I explain to my subordinates how his or her behavior affects the department and other employees?

___**43.** Did I explain to my subordinate why punitive discipline was necessary?

___**44.** When I administered discipline was I firm and not apologetic?

___**45.** Did I make sure my subordinate understood why discipline was necessary?

___**46.** Did I suggest how my subordinate could improve his or her behavior, attitude, work performance, and/or competence?

___**47.** Will discipline prevent a recurrence of the offense by the same subordinate?

___**48.** Have I considered the subordinate's prior conduct record, length of service, and past work performance?

___**49.** Have I indicated to my subordinate that no grudge will be held against him or her in the future?

___**50.** Have I indicated to my subordinate that future violations or a repeat of the same infraction will not be viewed lightly?

___**51.** Am I prepared to effectively deal with any resentment shown by the subordinate during the interview?

___**52.** Did I close the discussion with some expression of faith and confidence in my subordinate?

___**53.** Did I offer to shake hands with the subordinate at the conclusion of the interview?

___**54.** Can I defend myself and my actions against the union's charges, and more particularly with my superiors?

___**55.** Will I take time to make the necessary follow-up with my subordinate?

___**56.** If I feel that corrective action must be taken to improve the flow of work, or change or adjust a company policy which was the possible reason for the rule violation, will I make suggestions and recommendations to do so?

___**57.** If after a period of time, the subordinate does good work, will I compliment him or her, and do it in such a manner that it does not appear that I am trying to make up for my past disciplinary actions?

___**58.** Can I do everything possible to overcome any resentment on the part of the subordinate toward me, and resentment on my part toward the subordinate?

___**59.** Am I satisfied that my handling of the situation will have a sound effect on the attitudes and performance of the whole group?

___**60.** Will I do the same things in the future that I did when handling this disciplinary case?

___**61.** Will I spend an adequate amount of time analyzing this experience, and reflecting upon what was said and done on my part as well as on the part of the subordinate? (This should be considered as part of my self-development program as a manager.)

___**62.** Finally, what did I learn from this experience that will make me a more successful manager?_____

_____

_____

_____

7 HANDLING PROBLEM EMPLOYEES

Discretionary Management

A problem employee usually carries a burden of trouble(s) that directly and seriously interferes with job performance. In a very large sense, everyone could be considered a "problem employee," because all of us have our share of tensions, worries, unhappiness, anxieties, fears, suspicions, and temper. And we all act and react to such feelings and emotions to some extent both on and off the job.

There are differences, however, in how people handle their problems, their behavior associated with the problem, and how others perceive this overt behavior. It reminds me of the old fable about the two Quakers who were discussing life and people in general. One Quaker concluded the discussion by saying to the other, "Everyone's strange but thee and me—and even thee's a wee bit strange!" The question is, how and when do you as a manager decide that one of your subordinates is acting "strange" on the job? What do you look for? What symptoms are evident? But most important, what action should you take?

Defining on-the-job problem behavior

On-the-job problem behavior may be defined as those patterns of work behavior which cause an employee to fail to meet reasonable production standards. Production standards in this case refers to the amount of work expected to be produced in either office or plant environments. The key words or phrases in this definition are, "patterns of work behavior," "to fail," and "to meet reasonable."

Since work is a natural form of human behavior, the same as sleep, play, eating, and socializing, all of us develop habits and patterns of behavior which are identifiable and can be loosely classified by others, especially managers. When a sudden and/or prolonged change takes place in a subordinate's work behavior patterns, the experienced and successful manager is quick to notice it. A few examples of changed work behavior patterns are continued tardiness or excessive absences, frequent and long periods of idleness, continued failure to cooperate with others, an excessive amount and display of temper tantrums, continued irritability with others, increased sarcasm, unwillingness to accept authority, and excessive dependency upon others for help.

Although it is true that any one of us may display these symptoms temporarily at any time in our work career, that does not necessarily mean we are problem employees. It is the sudden change and/or prolonged unmistakable change in one's work behavior patterns that should be of concern to today's managers. Furthermore, when this type of a behavior change directly causes a subordinate to fail to meet his or her reasonable production standards, managers must take action.

One of the most vital aspects of human work life is that subordinates spend more time during their waking hours with their superiors than they do with anyone else. During any five-day, 40-hour work period, and in almost any type of job (there are exceptions), subordinates spend more time in face-to-face relationships with their superiors than they do with their husbands, wives, or other members of their immediate circle. Is it any wonder, then, that a vast number of subordinates seek out their immediate supervisor or manager to confide in? Propinquity spawns intimacy!

Managerial involvement

The one question that has confronted managers down through the years is, "How far should I get involved in my employee's problems?" Let me give you some basic guidelines.

A manager should not become involved with a subordinate's personal problems, as long as the problem does not interfere with his or her work or job performance. Many employees, including managers, have personal problems outside their work and job areas, but they do not permit these problems to interfere with their occupations and work responsibilities. Many employees actually look forward to going to work to escape the myriad problems that confront them at home.

Don't offer unsolicited advice no matter how well meant it may be. Too often this is resented by subordinates as meddling in their private affairs. Managers must keep in mind that certain people perform exceedingly well and receive personal satisfaction on their job, and yet suffer pain and torment outside the work area. To these people, their job means more than work and pay. In many cases it presents the one true opportunity to satisfy deep-seated needs for competition, creativity, recognition, achievement, and security, as well as to establish limited friendships and wholesome social relationships with fellow workers. For such an individual, the job may be the only part of his or her life that is a pleasure and not a problem. Therefore, any unsolicited advice or questioning about an employee's outside activities by a manager may be perceived as a threat not only to the individual's job security, but to the one positive and rewarding activity of that person's life. There are times, however, when you should take the initiative and talk to a subordinate about a situation both you and the employee recognize as a behavioral change that is influencing his or her work. Tell the individual that you are personally concerned about his or her problem, and that if necessary you want to help, if only to refer him or her to a qualified professional individual.

If a subordinate requests your time to discuss a personal problem, then set aside a time when both you and the employee can discuss the matter privately. This is good strategy on a manager's part, because whether you can help the employee or not, you act as a sounding board by permitting the employee to share his or her problems with someone else. This situation should also indicate to you that the subordinate has some degree of respect and confidence in your judgment. In a sense, it binds you and your subordinate more closely together.

Never lend money to subordinates, unless it is a dire emergency. Instead, suggest a bank or financial institution to solve the financial need without getting yourself involved.

Stay at arm's length when discussing domestic problems with your subordinates. This includes everything from separation and divorce to children and sexual incompatibility. Too many managers who have perceived themselves as well-wishers have ended up in court as the innocent, third-party victims.

Do not overprotect a subordinate who you suspect has a mental health problem, and do not be reluctant to take action in the employee's best interest.

Above all, don't play psychiatrist. In the first place, you're not trained in psychiatry, and second, you can cause more damage than you can cure. There are plenty of professional counselors, bona fide psychiatrists, ministers, priests, and rabbis who are better equipped to help than you are.

If you're in doubt about what to do, or what course of action to take, because of a lack of experience, or because it's a new or different situation, always consult with your superior.

Ask, listen, and act

When on-the-job problem behavior causes employees to fail to meet their production or work standards, the manager must intercede. But what must managers do, and how can they help?

Basically, the way to attempt to handle problem employees in any situation that you feel has a reasonable explanation is to ask the employee about it in private. Not all employees can or will, however, explain to their managers what's on their minds, or what's bothering them. Some people cannot express their feelings as well as others. Others fear they might jeopardize their relationship with their manager by saying something that may be interpreted as criticism, or make them appear in their manager's mind as weaklings, incapable of handling personal problems. I've always found that if subordinates like you, or trust you, and know from past experiences of your personal concern for other group members, they probably will open up. This is not a guarantee, however. There are those who will never open up, and for any number of personal reasons.

If individuals refuse to discuss the problem, which is their prerogative, then the only recourse you have is to state that you are aware of their deficient performance. Do not threaten, at this point, to use punitive discipline. Instead, show that you are personally concerned about the the employee, and will provide whatever help you can in the future, if he or she wishes to discuss the matter with you. At this point, conclude the meeting; thank your subordinate but remind him or her again that if you can help in some way, you will.

If the subordinate opens up and wishes to discuss his or her problem, your listening skills must be of the highest quality. You should not expect, however, that listening, or acting sympathetic, or reassuring employees that you know what they're going through will cure a deep-seated emotional problem. Some may break down and cry, which may be the best medicine at the moment. When a person cries, I encourage him or her to cry and cry hard, because this seems to temporarily relieve an internal pressure build-up.

Managers should also offer any practical help or advice within their power, especially if employees ask for it. This might include suggesting a professional counselor, family physician, or a clergyman if these seem appropriate. If your organization has a plant or staff physician or nurse, you might first consult with them and/or suggest that your employee visit them.

Whatever course of action the individual accepts should be confidential between you and the employee. However, to protect yourself as a manager, I would strongly suggest that you keep your superior informed of what happened, what you did, what you said, what the employee plans to do, and continue to follow up with periodic reports. Under no circumstances should you carry this burden and responsibility on your own shoulders, for several reasons.

If the employee recovers to a normal productive state, you should be commended for your action and help. But if the situation worsens and you have never confided with your superior, you could be justifiably castigated by those above you. Terminations and other disruptions within your group, as a result of improper action or no action on your part, could label you as an immature, irresponsible, and heartless manager.

If the problem should reach a point where the individual commits suicide at work or at home, or goes berserk at work, the consequences could permanently damage your reputation and work career. Families of the victim have sued organizations for much less, and supervisors and managers have been shot down in cold blood in similar situations.

Finally, the reason organizations have constructed hierarchies is to share mutual management problems up and down the so-called chain of command. Don't be foolish and try to play hero, when in essence you might end up being the goat. You have superiors—use them!

Handling the alcoholic employee

No organization is immune to the possibility of alcoholism among some of its employees. Recently a well-known Pittsburgh psychiatrist, Dr. Abraham Twerski, speaking at the Pittsburgh Personnel Association's all-day conference, referred to the "epidemic of escapism" sweeping the nation. (Dr. Twerski is the Clinical Director of the Department of Psychiatry at St. Francis Hospital, and Medical Director of the Gateway Rehabilitation Center in Aliquippa, Pennsylvania.) Dr. Twerski said,

Drugs and alcohol are merely methods of escaping, and when an individual cannot deal with reality, then escape becomes necessary. If a person feels he is greater than the challenge, he will cope with it, and if the challenge is greater than [he is, he] escapes. . . . The greatest source of difficulty is in a person's underestimating his own capabilities, rather than overestimating the challenge. If you see yourself as inadequate, then you'll try to escape every challenge. Two of these escape mechanisms are alcohol and drugs.*

* *The Pittsburgh Press,* May 19, 1978.

A TRAINING PROGRAM FOR MANAGERS AND SUPERVISORS

The following article was written to present to industrial training personnel a logical, systematic, and realistic training technique that could be incorporated into a management development training program.*

This outline is intended to be flexible enough so that small, medium, and large companies can use it as a guide. It certainly is not the last word, nor is it intended to be.

1. *Statement of Company Policy*
Simply stated, your company regards alcoholism among its employees as an illness which is treatable. Define alcoholism and explain the purpose of the policy.

1A. *Supervisor's Responsibility*
Since the company's concern with alcoholism is strictly limited to its effects on the *employee's performance of his or her job*, the supervisor or manager must be held responsible for the implementation of the policy, by following a set of predetermined procedures.

1B. *Employees' Responsibility*
Employees will be encouraged to seek diagnosis, comply with diagnostic referrals, and cooperate with prescribed therapy. This illness will be handled in the same manner as any other, nonalcoholic illness. All cases will be handled in confidence, and the implementation of the policy requires no special regulations, privileges, or exemptions from the standard administrative practices now in existence and applicable to any employee's normal job performance requirements.

2. *Administration*
This spells out by job title who in the company will have the total responsibility for the operation of the program.

3. *Procedure*
This focuses on certain pretreatment functions through coordinated efforts of management and union personnel. These functions include:

A. Creation of a plantwide climate through generalized education pro-

* Paul W. Cummings, "Handling the Alcoholic Employee—A Supervisor's Training Program," *Training and Development Journal*, February 1975, pp. 42–44. Copyright 1975 by the American Society for Training and Development, Inc. Reproduced by special permission.

cesses—the distribution of free literature to attempt to reduce the social stigma associated with alcoholism.

B. Enlisting the cooperation and support of the local union organization.

C. Identifying and motivating to treatment possible alcoholic cases where poor job performance is concerned.

D. Developing a follow-up program to assure procedures are being followed.

E. Scheduling initial and follow-up training meetings, pointing out the necessity of keeping records, observing behavior patterns, and formal and informal discipline action to be taken.

4. *Personnel Administration*

This outlines the basic role the Personnel Department will play, including labor relations involvement, cooperation with the union, and the fact that standard administrative procedures will be used.

5. *The Supervisor's or Manager's Role*

A. Supervisors and managers need to be alert and observe employee work performance especially when it fails to meet established work standards.

B. Supervisors and managers will document all specific instances of employees' behavior failing to meet these standards.

C. Supervisors and managers will conduct corrective interviews when substandard performance is warranted, and tell the employee the company is willing to offer counseling or diagnostic services to assist him or her. If the employee accepts, he or she will be referred to professional sources. In some cases this might be active members of Alcoholics Anonymous as well as certain local community agency resources.

D. If the employee refuses help, and his or her performance continues unsatisfactorily, he or she is given a firm choice between professional diagnosis once again, or accepting existing disciplinary procedures usually exercised for all cases of unsatisfactory job performance.

E. Supervisors and managers should not "play doctor" by attempting to diagnose the cause, nor should they discuss "drinking problems" with employees under their direction. Supervisors and managers should refrain from writing the diagnosis or supposition that an employee has alcoholism on any company forms. Finally, a supervisor or manager should not terminate a previously satisfactory employee for unsatisfactory performance before giving the employee appropriate opportunities to seek assistance.

6. *The Role of Training*

This program is based entirely on employee job performance. It requires keeping records and data by management when evaluating employees, as well as a knowledge of interviewing techniques when appraising the employee in private. The line foreman must be instructed to keep the channels of communication open, both upward and downward, including appropriate staff personnel. The number of times a supervisor or manager is required to schedule a job performance appraisal interview in private is dependent upon the employee's behavior, acceptance or rejection of assistance, the nature of his or her job, advice of superiors, etc.

Thus, role-playing, "buzz" sessions, interpersonal grievance procedure reviews are excellent subject matters for supervisory conferences related to alcoholism. Each supervisor or manager should be given a list of on-the-job signs of progressive alcoholism, since once drinking is unmistakably identified and related to the performance problem, the illness has usually reached a middle stage, especially among the blue collar employees. A brief review of treatment and recovery services provided by local community agencies will enlarge the supervisor's or manager's understanding of the totality of this problem.

Finally, the supervisor and/or manager should be made aware of labor and management's coordinated efforts to achieve their mutual objective, the employee's restoration to good health and productivity. This is necessary and vital to the success of a program of this nature.

In response to this article, Michael R. Omelanuk wrote a letter to the editor of the *Training and Development Journal,** in which he added some ideas:

Here are suggestions derived from experience which should prove beneficial to other trainers.

Brief your upper management but train the supervisors first. If you start training at the top, management will expect supervisors to cope with situations for which they have not been trained. It is far easier to convert individual managers when a situation surfaces in their area than to deal with the frustrations of the supervisor.

Be sure that the person who will be your referral or treatment agent is present during the training. If you do not, you the trainer will become the referral point. Supervisors will be thinking of you as the resident expert.

* April 1975, p. 57.

Team teaching is indicated here. You can never hope to match the knowledge of an outside expert on alcohol (most states provide this service free), but he can never answer the questions applicable to your company's work force and policies.

Be sure that your organization is ready for action in this area. You will get referrals almost immediately.

Train union representatives and supervisors together. Since cooperation is the key factor, all conflicts can be surfaced and resolved in class. In this way there will be no suspicions that management is "after" a particular worker.

Remember that supervisors can also be alcoholics. When you have your first supervisor referred, you have passed a significant milestone.

THE SYMPTOMS OF THE ALCOHOLIC EMPLOYEE

One of the problems for managers in dealing with the alcoholic employee is that in the early stages it is very difficult to detect. Individuals in the early stages are very clever at hiding their illness, and most will avoid medical or other forms of professional help. Furthermore, by the time a manager suspects an employee of being alcoholic, the illness is usually in a middle or advanced stage.

The manager must recognize that alcoholics differ. Some exhibit most of the symptoms listed below, while others exhibit only a few. To further complicate the problem, managers must realize that personal problems (family, finances, or personal traumas), or certain diseases other than alcoholism (a heavy chest cold), may tend to cause certain of the symptoms of early alcoholism, and finally, not everyone who exhibits these symptoms is an alcoholic. This is why a correct diagnosis can be made only by a physician, not by a supervisor or manager. Therefore, let's examine the more common symptoms of alcoholism.

1. Constant alcoholic odor on the breath.
2. Very frequent absences on a Monday, or the day following payday.
3. An unsteady gait, or shaky hands.
4. An uneven work pace that becomes increasingly slower.
5. A steady decline in work performance coupled with alibis for failure, in which case others are blamed.

6. Shifting of moods from euphoria to depression and perhaps faulty memory.
7. Frequent and long trips to the rest room.
8. Consistent minor traffic accidents and/or charges of careless or drunken driving by local police officials.
9. A noticeable degree of "thick-tongued speech," bloodshot eyes, or a flushed face.

These common symptoms are merely guidelines to help the manager detect employees who may be beyond the entry-level stage of alcoholism.

THE ALCOHOLIC EXECUTIVE

What symptoms or behavior patterns would a middle manager use to detect an alcoholic executive, especially if the executive happened to be his or her immediate superior? Some of the usual lower-level-employee symptoms such as frequent absenteeism after a weekend or payday, lower job performance, and even longer lunch hours are not necessarily ironclad symptoms. Since executives have rank and power, they are craftier than the average employee in covering up a drinking problem. Unfortunately, because of the rank executives enjoy, they are often protected by fellow employees and secretaries. In many cases these subordinates have no other choice, or are fearful of discussing the boss's problem with the boss.

Different behavior patterns which may be alcoholic symptoms that only executives can display would include increased or extravagant expense account charges, early arrivals and/or late departures at company functions involving free liquor, and extreme marital problems. An alcoholic executive cannot escape, however, regardless of rank, the telltale physical symptoms such as bloodshot eyes, unusual gait, alcoholic breath, thick-tongued speech, vacillating moods, and a flushed face, to mention a few.

The burning question, however, is what do you do when your superior's superior questions you, a middle manager, about your boss's suspected alcoholism? Do you protect your boss? Do you play dumb and deny any knowledge of your boss's illness? Or do you help your boss by admitting some degree of knowledge of his or her illness?

When the question was asked of me, I chose the third, and in time, with professional help and understanding, the individual recovered.

THE AERP PROGRAM

The Alcoholic Employee Rehabilitation Program (AERP) is another successful technique that many organizations are using today. An interesting and informative article by August Ralston* noted that the AERP technique was developed not only to rehabilitate alcoholic employees, but to reduce the cost of employee alcoholism. The surge in the development of AERPs reflects an evolution in personnel policy. Many companies are discovering that the initial response to an alcoholic employee should not be termination. Instead, various programs such as the AERP have been organized to offer employees professional assistance so that they can overcome their problems, keep their jobs, and continue to be productive. It should also be noted that unions have been influential in starting AERPs.

The supervisor or manager starts the rehabilitation process by documenting the deterioration in work performance. In an initial interview with the employee, the manager suggests that excessive drinking may be the problem. If the condition is not corrected within a short time, the manager will offer referral to medical and staff advisers, or if the employee's value to the company is questionable, he or she may be terminated. Disciplinary action is withheld if referral is accepted.

The initial step of the medical services staff is to evaluate the condition of the employee. If rehabilitation is advisable and if the employee agrees to cooperate, an assistance program is planned for the employee. The role of the medical services and advisory staffs in the AERP is to guide the employee to various outside sources of assistance and to supervise the process of rehabilitation. The AERP is not an in-house program. The recommended rehabilitation program may involve a family doctor, clergyman, rehabilitation center, the employee's family, and Alcoholics Anonymous.

The alcoholic employee is not always rehabilitated. If the employee shows evidence of satisfactory progress, occasional relapses

*"Employee Alcoholism: Response of the Largest Industrials," *The Personnel Administrator*, August 1977, pp. 50–56.

may be tolerated and disciplinary action is deferred. However, the threat of discipline is instrumental to the success of rehabilitation. Employees of industrial organizations, in general, are more responsive than others to rehabilitation in problem drinking cases. They are often long-service employees whose job pride and the fear of losing the job provide strong motivation for rehabilitation. Disciplinary action may include suspension, demotion, forced retirement, or termination.

Alcoholics are not cured; they have the disease till they die. Therefore, the recovery or rehabilitation of an alcoholic employee cannot be considered a cure. Instead, a measure of recovery must be applied which relates to work performance. It is implicit that employees are not rehabilitated unless they are performing to the satisfaction of their supervisors' or managers' expectations.

THE DIRECT APPROACH

Confronting an alcoholic employee directly and stating that he or she cannot keep up the present conduct and continue to work for the organization may seem brutal, but this direct approach serves three basic purposes for both the manager and the employee:

First, it confronts the employee with a reality—that his or her job is in jeopardy. Second, it supports and maintains that thread of the employee's personality that tells him or her that it is necessary to kick the habit of alcoholism. In essence, the employee wants to break away from the misery and high cost of drinking. As a partially recovered alcoholic employee once told me, "I knew I had a problem, but I needed someone else to tell me and help me." Finally, it gives you a means of identifying and handling an employee's problem objectively. It also helps you, the manager, to ease your anxiety feelings about avoiding the issue. In effect, it puts the problem right where it belongs—out in the open.

SUMMARY

Here are chronological and positive steps that a manager can take to help an alcoholic employee:

1. When you suspect an employee of becoming alcoholic, review his or her production and attendance records.

2. Talk to the employee. Ask for explanations, and don't be satisfied with misleading answers. Seek the diagnosis of a physician to establish the fact that alcohol is the problem.
3. Explain the seriousness of the problem to the employee, and that you can refer him or her to professional sources.
4. Suggest that the employee take a leave of absence, if necessary.
5. Assure the employee that he or she will have a job if help is obtained; otherwise the employee will not be retained.
6. If the employee agrees to seek help and your organization has a procedure established, refer the employee to the individual who is responsible for administering the program.
7. As a manager, don't back off. Once you and the employee decide on a course of action, follow through. The alcoholic is mentally conditioned to empty threats and/or promises. He or she needs to understand that you are willing to help, but you also mean business if he or she fails to seek help.
8. Assure the alcoholic employee that when he or she has recovered, you and fellow employees will be supportive and encouraging when the employee returns to work.

Handling drug abuse

Management's approach toward the drug abuse employee is more difficult to administer than the approach normally taken for other unusual employee behavior such as alcoholism, gambling, personal problems, or emotional illness. Drug usage itself may refer to a wide variety of substances ranging from over-the-counter tranquilizers to prescribed pharmaceuticals, illegal materials such as heroin, LSD, and "angel dust." On the surface, handling drug abuse and alcoholism may appear to be similar, but there are important and significant differences between the two.

First, alcohol can be legally obtained, while many of the hallucinatory and/or "hard" narcotic-type drugs must be obtained illegally.

Second, a substantial amount of alcohol must be carried or transported in containers, such as bottles or metal flasks, and can only be consumed orally. Many, but not all, drugs can be concealed on a person's body, or in clothing, wallet, or purse, since only a small dosage is required to get high. Thus, drugs are much easier to carry or transport to one's workplace than alcohol. Certain drugs need not be taken orally.

Third, the consumption of alcohol must be done privately at work, in hidden and secluded locations. Closets, hallways, or rest rooms may serve the purpose, but many times the odor of alcohol lingers on for several minutes. Drugs and certain pills, on the other hand, can be "popped" at an individual's desk, workbench, at the water cooler, or in an office where others are working, and there are no telltale traces such as the odor of alcohol.

Fourth, the alcoholic employee seldom involves other employees in his or her habit while on the job. Drug abusers, on the other hand, have a greater tendency to want to share their habit with other employees. This is especially true of the younger employees from age eighteen to twenty-five. This is known as the "contamination fear theory" by management, because the drug abuser may introduce, infect, and consequently contaminate other employees.

Fifth, once the drug abuse employee is well "hooked," his or her habit becomes more expensive than the alcoholic's. Thus, in order to pay for his or her daily drug habit, the drug abuser may steal valuable company property or sell company secrets.

Finally, there is usually, but not always, more sympathy and understanding for the person with an alcohol hangover, because most nonalcoholic employees have experienced this phenomenon sometime in their lives. The drug abuse employee is relatively new to American business and industry, and management has a lot to learn about handling this type of a problem employee.

COMMON SYMPTOMS OF THE DRUG ABUSE EMPLOYEE

Again, the responsibility for detecting the drug abuse employee falls upon the supervisor or manager. Some of the more common symptoms are:

1. Frequent unexplained absences from the job.
2. Frequent lateness when reporting to work, and sudden requests to leave work early for no apparent reasons.

3. An unusually high frequency of visits to the rest room. Sudden disappearances from his or her work station coupled with unauthorized visitations to other parts of an office building or plant.

4. Reports by other employees of unusual, but temporary, behavior.

5. A sudden increase in the theft of valuable company property, such as precious metals or office equipment.

6. Sudden and frequent requests for pay advances or company loans, or excessive requests to borrow money from fellow employees.

7. Sudden and unexplainable fluctuations in work performance.

8. An unusually high frequency of minor accidents whose origins and causes are extremely difficult to investigate.

9. Observance of consistent, abnormally dilated or constricted pupils in an employee's eyes. This is very difficult to observe, however, because many individuals wear automatically adjusting tinted lenses rather than clear, nontinted lenses.

10. Unusual behavior, such as excessive talkativeness, loud speech, unsteadiness in body movements or gait, drowsiness, or sometimes difficulty in coordinating hand movements.

A TRAINING PROGRAM FOR HANDLING
THE DRUG ABUSE EMPLOYEE

The training program outlined below* is designed to be flexible so that small, medium, and large work organizations can use it as a guide. While it may lack completeness for your specific needs, it provides a framework upon which the reader may build.

Statement of Company Policy
The company believes in . . . the following:

1. Drug abuse is an illness.

2. The drug abuser can be helped to recover.

3. The company is willing to offer assistance.

4. It must be the employee's decision to seek diagnosis and accept treatment when his or her *job performance* can be proved to be:

*The training program outlined here is reprinted from Cummings, "A Supervisor's Training Program for Handling the Drug Abuse Employee," *Journal of Continuing Education and Training*, December 1971, pp. 181–190.

(a) Substandard.

(b) The direct result of drug abuse.

5. If the drug abuse employee refuses to make the decision to seek diagnosis and accept treatment, and his or her job performance continues to be substandard, he or she faces the possibility of termination based on the following discipline criteria:

(a) Number of past drug abuse occurrences.

(b) Severity of the offense.

(c) The degree of danger involved to himself and others including damage to company property.

(d) The degree to which state and federal laws have been violated.

(e) Any other medical considerations relevant to his or her drug abuse.

6. The company further believes in early diagnosis and treatment and this to be done in confidence.

Manager's and Supervisor's Responsibility

The company's concern with drug abuse is strictly limited to its effects on the *employee's performance of his or her job.* However, any employee convicted of . . . illegal drug traffic charges, either on company premises during working hours, or after the employee's scheduled work hours, in or out of the plant, will be terminated.

Employees' Responsibility

Employees will be encouraged to make the decision to seek diagnosis and co-operate with the prescribed therapy. The employee's illness will be handled in the same manner as any other, non-drug-abuse illness. All cases will be handled in strict confidence, and the implementation of the policy requires no special regulations, privileges, or exemptions from the standard administrative practices now in existence and applicable to any employee's normal job performance requirements.

1. Personal leaves of absence will be arranged for rehabilitation purposes, and follow-up measures will be taken to insure that the employee continues treatment and does not revert back to drugs again.

2. The employee should understand that if the medical opinion for rehabilitation is negative, or if he continues drug usage, or rejects treatment, or returns to drugs, he or she will be permanently dismissed.

3. The use of drugs or narcotics will become a permanent entry in an employee's personal file and will also be maintained in the personnel department permanent record.

4. Applicants who admit the illicit use of drugs will not be considered for employment; however, those who can show satisfactory evidence of recovery from drug abuse will not be discriminated against.

Administration
This part of the training program should spell out by job title who in the company will have the total responsibility for the operation of the program.

Procedure
This should focus on certain functions and coordinated efforts of management and union personnel. These to include:

1. Enlist and maintain the cooperation and support of the local union organization.

2. Create a favorable plantwide climate through generalized education processes. Distribute free literature to attempt to reduce the social stigma associated [with] drug abuse. Primarily, education should be synonymous with drug abuse prevention.

3. Identify and motivate drug abuse employees to be diagnosed and treated. Identification to be made on the basis of *poor job performance*.

4. Develop a follow-up program to assure procedures are being carried out.

5. Schedule initial and follow-up training meetings with management, pointing out the necessity of keeping records, observing behavior patterns, and formal and informal disciplinary action to be taken.

6. Special problems:
   (a) Drug identification—If drugs are found the manager has two choices to follow: check the drugs with a local pharmacist; present the material to your local police department.
   (b) Search and seizure—If drugs are suspected of being in a locker or desk, make sure of the legality of your actions. You may want to develop an entire search and seizure procedure.
   (c) Hiring procedures—May have to be re-evaluated in terms of physical examinations, individuals on prescription drugs (the diabetic), and probationary period job behavior.
   (d) Marijuana—Until such time that the AMA and the American Bar Association, as well as the various courts, rule in favor of or against the use of marijuana, the policy will be to consider it an illegal drug or an intoxicant (the same as alcohol), and subject to the provisions of this total program.

Personnel Administration

This part of the training program should outline the basic role the Personnel Department will play. This should include:

1. Union-management cooperation.

2. Labor relations involvement, from grievances to arbitration to civil court action.

3. The creation, use, and maintenance of standard administrative procedures.

The Manager's and Supervisor's Role

1. Managers and supervisors must be alert and observe employee work performance, especially when it fails to meet established work standards.

2. Managers and supervisors will document all specific instances of employee behavior failing to meet these standards.

3. Managers and supervisors will immediately conduct a private corrective interview with the drug abuser when substandard performance is evident and it is clearly the result of self-administered drugs.

Content of the discussion by the supervisor should cover the following:

(a) Awareness of the employee's drug abuse problem through poor job performance.

(b) The company and management consider it an illness.

(c) The company and management are willing to help the individual, but the employee must make the decision to seek diagnosis and therapy.

(d) If the employee accepts help he or she will be referred to professional outside sources and local community agency resources.

4. If employees refuse help, or deny their drug abusiveness, or deny that poor job performance is the result of drug abusiveness, they should be given a firm choice once again between seeking professional diagnosis, or accepting existing disciplinary procedures normally exercised for all cases of unsatisfactory job performance.

5. Managers and supervisors should not "play doctor" by attempting to diagnose the cause of the drug abuser's problem. Nor should the manager or supervisor become involved in "bush-league" detective work as a result of reading well-meaning and well-illustrated pamphlets [with] colored pictures of pills, capsules, powders, and equipment. It is the deviant employee behavior causing substandard job performance that should concern the supervisor.

6. Supervisors and managers should refrain from writing a diagnosis or personal supposition on any company forms.

7. A supervisor or manager should not terminate a previously satisfactory employee for unsatisfactory performance before giving the employee appropriate opportunities to seek assistance.

The Role of Training

This program is based entirely on *employee job performance*. The employee's performance must be satisfactory as defined by meeting the established work standards of the office, department, or plant of the company or corporation in which this program is to be installed.

1. Training must do the following for managers, supervisors, and forepersons:

(a) Teach management how to keep simple yet efficient records and data on their employees.

(b) Train management to properly evaluate their employees.

(c) Teach management interviewing techniques to help them appraise employees in private, and increase their communication skills which are needed when communicating both up and down.

2. Training specialists must consider using other methods and techniques for the purpose of providing their managers with insight into the drug abuser problem. Some of these methods are:

(a) Audiovisual aids and equipment (films, etc.).

(b) Lectures on drug identification and health by outside experts.

(c) Other training methods such as role playing, "buzz" sessions, and a review of the grievance procedure.

3. Whenever possible, training should teach its managers how to detect the use of illegal drugs on the job. (Example—duplicate the odor of marijuana.)

4. It should also stress the drug traffic procedure, that is, how it is set up and maintained by employees in the plant.

5. Training should make managers and supervisors aware of the coordinated efforts of the local labor union and the company in achieving their mutual objectives, that is, the employee's restoration to good health and productivity. Management may want to consider the use of a union-management "ombudsman" approach to this and other deviant behavior problems.

The ombudsman approach

Ombudsman is the title of an appointed official who is given special powers to receive, investigate, and report alleged grievances and complaints both in and out of government.

The concept has been used widely in Europe and the Scandinavian countries for years, and is slowly becoming more popular in the United States, especially in industry and business. Chrysler Corporation, for instance, uses an ombudsman to handle customer complaints; two Kentucky newspapers, *The Courier-Journal* and the *Louisville Times,* have installed the program to handle by telephone thousands of customer suggestions, complaints, or compliments. In the early 1970s, Grumman Aerospace Corporation, a nonunion organization, used the ombudsman approach as a substitute for union shop stewards and/or grievancemen. Within companies, the ombudsman functions best in large and medium-size corporations that are nonunion.

The main role of the ombudsman is to be a good listener and interested in employees and their problems. The ombudsman acts as a referral point and helps the company keep a human dimension. Often employees are reluctant to bring problems and complaints to their immediate supervisors, but are willing to discuss their problems confidentially with an ombudsman. Essentially, ombudsmen do not solve problems, but refer problems—small and large, work-related and personal—to the personnel relations department.

The ombudsman is an extension of an organization's total communication system. Some of the larger organizations have employed several ombudsmen whose work has led to the creation of review boards who work in conjunction with the personnel department and handle terminations, promotion requests, skill development, various community and public relations efforts, alleged discriminations, questions about pay raises, pensions, and retirements.

Is the ombudsman technique successful? It will only be as successful as management wants it to be. If large, nonunion organizations, such as service and manufacturing companies, are desirous of keeping organized labor out of its formal structure, perhaps an ombudsman program might achieve this goal.

Techniques for handling personal problems

Described below is a brief technique managers should consider using when handling personal problems.

Maintain your objectivity. Whenever managers want to help subordinates or peer group members, they must be able to understand
how the other person feels, and *why* he or she feels a given way.

Distinguish clearly between those problems you can and wish to
help with and those that are impossible to solve even though you
would like to be of assistance to the individual. No one can ever solve
someone else's problem, but it is often possible to *help* individuals
solve their own problems by maintaining objectivity, and by helping
them to articulate and communicate how they really feel. By encouraging and permitting individuals to talk, you may help them to separate feelings from facts. Once the individual can separate objective reality from emotions, help the person develop and examine various
courses of action that can be taken.

Managers must realize that compassion for others is a normal psychological feeling. In fact, controlled compassion should be part of a
manager's personal makeup. Furthermore, there is nothing weak or
wrong about feeling sorry for individual subordinates and wanting to
help them.

Handling the marginal worker

The marginal worker is the one whose work is below an acceptable level, or who repeatedly falls from satisfactory to unsatisfactory
performance. Therefore, the first thing a manager must do is to objectively identify those factors that constitute marginality of a subordinate. Once you have established a standardized system for making this
evaluation, conduct private interviews to *tell* your subordinates about
their marginal performance and that improvement is expected. Next,
ask these individuals how they can improve their performance, and
what you can expect from them in the future.

The problem with most managers is that they never communicate
their dissatisfaction to subordinates about their marginal performance. Many managers simply lack the courage to tell or ask
marginal employees to improve. But managerial responsibility doesn't
end there. Once the individual understands you're dissatisfied with
his or her performance, and accepts that fact, it then becomes your
responsibility to train, counsel, and coach the individual. You must

provide every opportunity for improvement, and this requires patience.

Many managers have done a lot of disservice to their subordinates, to their work units, and to their organizations by stringing subordinates along and hoping that they will catch on, improve, or straighten out. Managers must confront the problem directly.

I've witnessed a classical case where a plant manager had his personnel manager so confused and befuddled that, no matter what the personnel manager did or said, it was judged to be wrong. But with a little patience, understanding, and constructive help on the plant manager's part, the personnel manager could have been salvaged. The poor personnel manager's actions and reactions were being negatively read, discussed, and evaluated by everyone in the plant, and as usual, in a few months the personnel manager was let go.

Who was right and who was wrong in this case? I would say that the plant manager and the personnel manager were both wrong. Whoever was responsible for hiring the personnel manager in the first place made a bad decision, because the individual was ill-equipped to handle the job. Obviously, the plant manager made a bad situation worse by not confronting the individual, explaining his dissatisfaction, and making an honest attempt to counsel and coach his subordinate manager. The solution? Fire him! This was the easy way out for the plant manager—the road of least resistance—the road which too many managers choose to travel today.

What should have been done? The following successful techniques for handling a marginal manager should have been used:

1. Clarify your goals.
2. Discuss your goals and the marginal employee's goals.
3. Agree to combine both goals. Agree to agree, rather than to disagree.
4. Agree upon a plan of action which involves both you and the marginal employee.
5. Maintain your end of the agreement, and actively encourage improvement.
6. Continually evaluate progress being made.
7. Use a performance chart, or keep records so that the marginal

individual you are rehabilitating can see his or her performance and progress.

8. If after all this the mission fails, then you have a justifiable reason to terminate the marginal employee's services.

Handling the young employee

Significant differences in social values exist today between adults and their children. They may be expressed in dress, speech, behavior, ideals, and goals. Some of the problems associated with young employees whose values clash with the established values have included a lack of knowledge of how to perform manual labor, dissatisfaction with the type of job assignment and its pay, disregard for company property, nonadherence to basic company rules and regulations, and in some cases disrespect for authority as well as a high turnover rate for new employees.

A large manufacturing plant in western New York State conducted a research program in 1974 to gather an expression of various attitudes and opinions from a representative sample of the blue collar production employees. The purpose was to get a better understanding of their employees' needs and wishes so that several new employee-oriented programs could be installed. The following excerpt reflects several successful management techniques that should be practiced.

Thus far we have presented only the employees' points of view concerning their perception of their supervisors—and this from only one industrial plant. When it came time to review the results of this survey with the plant manager, it was suggested we hold supervisory conferences and openly discuss many of these employee reactions and opinions. We did this in a series of conferences, and changed the names and departments to protect those employees who had given honest appraisals.

During the course of these sessions we started to list all of the worthwhile suggestions the supervisors and managers made concerning how they felt they could best supervise the under-30 . . . employees. We would like to share these suggestions with you, our readers.

There are three attributes each supervisor and manager should strive for when dealing with the under-30 . . . employee.

1. Although it may sound glib or superficial, today's supervisors and managers must abstain from bias or prejudicial feelings based on their young employees' appearances. How an employee "looks" to you is secondary—*it's his or her performance that counts.* However, where safety, personal health, or cleanliness is concerned, you should, of course, exercise your supervisory prerogatives and responsibilities.

2. Our young employees are a tremendous human resource to be trained and developed, not ignored, or subtly abused in a work situation. The likelihood of an overnight change in life style or value structure is quite remote, but a fact that is even more difficult to contest is the continually increasing numbers of youth who will make up tomorrow's labor market.

3. Know your employees—yes, even the "longhairs"! Resolve your differences and personal feelings and reach an understanding by taking the initiative through the leadership which is vested in you. You must take the first step and lead the way if you want satisfactory working relations.

Finally, don't be a "square" when you supervise the longhair. And how do you do this? Practice some of these modern management skills:

1. *Don't label the longhair.* Longhairs don't need labeling from you—that's why they choose the appearance they do. In effect, they have labeled themselves and want it that way. This self-labeling process (longhair) they can accept—they don't need or want yours.

2. *Don't treat them like cold impersonal "check numbers."* They have names and they're human. Call them by their names and treat them as you would like to be treated if you had their job.

3. *Make them part of the organization.* Get them involved by giving them some degree of responsibility and simple decisions to make.

4. *Verbally communicate with them.* Listening doesn't mean you have to agree with their value structure and life style. Who knows—you might learn something about today's youth you didn't know before.

5. *Be honest and truthful* and give them the facts about work, their performance, or lack of it. Young people have their own opinions about things, and you're being paid to lead, not preach.

6. *Teach, don't preach.* The majority of youth want to learn, want to progress, want to get ahead. When you train them you are providing them with the necessary tools and equipment to achieve. Leave the preaching for others.

7. *Give them a challenge.* To some people, sweeping a floor can be a challenge. To others, it's a drag. When you as a supervisor have learned how to make sweeping a floor a challenge for your employees, you're well on your way to winning awards as the best supervisor in the plant.

8. *Lead, don't push.* Youth is extremely idealistic and respects those who truly lead, rather than con-men, manipulators, and factory, plant, or office politicians.

9. *Don't wear your rank on your sleeve.* Everyone in the plant knows who you are and what your status position is within the formal organization. Quite frankly, gentlemen, the "bull-of-the-woods" has been put to pasture!*

* Paul W. Cummings, "Don't Be a Square When You Supervise the Longhair," *Applied Training,* February 1974, pp. 8–18.

# **Motivation**

Managerial Inspiration

In this chapter, the reader will find three basic motivational techniques which I have used over the years with success. These techniques rely on employee participation and decision-making, recognition, and group motivational behavior patterns with emphasis on natural leader techniques. These three basic techniques encompass several subtechniques, written and developed in the form of inventories, any of which can be practiced at any particular time and in any type of work group or situation. For this chapter to be effective, you must carefully review each question in each inventory and determine if the question implies a course of action you may want to follow. The final section, on money as a motivator, is appropriate in this day and age. You may or may not agree with my conclusions in this last section.

Employee participation as a motivating force

As a manager in our contemporary work world you should permit and encourage subordinates to participate in setting departmental objectives as well as their own. This is especially true in their work activities and in the decisions affecting them. Basically, the motivating force is developed from the fact that there is *ownership* in injecting one's own ideas, values, and decisions into one's work. Ownership in this case means belonging to, pertaining to, or relating to one's self, through possession or proprietorship of the conduct, participation in, and decisions of the work in which one is engaged. As a manager, imagine if you can how little pride and sense of responsibility and accomplishment you would have if you did not make your own decisions and were not permitted to participate in various work activities within your own group.

Obviously, the degree of ownership must be limited and controlled somewhat, but when subordinates are given the opportunity to offer suggestions, or influence decisions in work activities affecting them, they are participating, and employee participation breeds positive motivation. The reasons why managers should consider using employee participation as a motivational technique relate to contemporary levels of employee education, the development of sophisticated work methods and labor-saving devices, and the need to have one's worth recognized.

The average level of education for most employees engaged in gainful permanent occupations has risen significantly today compared with 20 or 30 years ago. Today, employees are better prepared educationally when they join work organizations than their parents were one generation ago. They have learned certain skills, want to continue to learn, and wish to apply their learning on the job. What better place can employees fulfill this desire than at work?

Moreover, many work because methods have become highly technical and sophisticated today, they create natural challenges to individuals and groups. If these challenges and curiosities are not satisfied by employees who are required to use the newer methods and techniques, then only a minimum of both human and machine performance can be expected. Thus, management loses the maximum potential of its financial investment in the method as well as in the employee(s).

Respect for human dignity and the worth of each employee should make us aware of the difference between making employees actually important and simply making employees feel important. Making an employee feel important for a short period of time is too phony and temporary—what do you do for encores? On the other hand, making employees important is more consistent and lasting, and eventually brings about self-motivation, which brings out the best in people.

A MOTIVATIONAL INVENTORY FOR MEASURING EMPLOYEE PARTICIPATION

How effective are you in cultivating participation of employees in work activities and decisions affecting them? Read each question in this inventory and check the appropriate answer(s). Your own honest analysis should serve as a guide to how successful you are in this aspect of employee motivation.

How much authority do you permit your employees to exercise in the work activities and decisions affecting them?

___**1.** Complete authority

___**2.** Limited authority

___**3.** Little authority

___**4.** Absolutely none

How often do you hold formal group meetings with your employees to discuss the overall work activities of the group?

___**1.** Daily

___**2.** Once a week

___**3.** Twice a month

___**4.** Once a month

___**5.** Hardly ever

If and when you hold formal group meetings with your employees, which of the following statements best describes what takes place? (Check only those answers that apply.)

___ **1.** Meetings are usually short (less than 30 minutes).

___ **2.** My meetings are informative to everyone.

___ **3.** Meetings are usually long (one hour or more).

___ **4.** Everyone has an opportunity to speak, but some do not.

___ **5.** I seek and discuss ideas and suggestions during the meeting.

___ **6.** I encourage everyone to speak up sometime during the meeting and most of them do.

___ **7.** I feel my agenda and subject content are well balanced.

___ **8.** Most of the time the meetings are productive.

___ **9.** Each individual is given an assignment and is expected to report back at the next meeting.

___**10.** I rotate the chairperson at each meeting.

___**11.** About half the time the meeting is a gripe session.

___**12.** I encourage my employees to openly discuss past, present, and future work problems.

___**13.** Individual assignments made at the last meeting are brought up and discussed.

___**14.** I table very few sensitive issues.

___**15.** All meetings are briefly summarized before concluding so that participants know their assignments and responsibilities.

If your employees have an idea for improving their work, what must take place before they can initiate and incorporate the idea into their procedures?

___**1.** They are required to get my approval.

___**2.** They go ahead and make the change so long as it doesn't interfere with the entire operation of my department or with other employees' procedures and production.

___**3.** I encourage all my employees to make all necessary changes or job improvements, without my immediate approval, so long as quality, safety, and production standards are not abandoned.

___**4.** They must fill out a company form and submit it to me. I review it first, and if it looks suitable it's reviewed by several committees, such as engineering and safety. After a period of time the idea is either accepted or rejected.

___**5.** Most of my employees make changes or job improvements that I don't know about.

___**6.** Generally, most of my employees don't make changes or try to improve their job procedures. They know it would be too much trouble to go through.

___**7.** I make all the job improvements in my department.

If an employee suddenly experiences a difficult work problem, what does he or she generally do?

___**1.** Comes to me and asks for help.

___**2.** Goes to a fellow employee and seeks help.

___**3.** Tries to work around the problem.

___**4.** Does nothing.

___**5.** Tries to solve the problem as best he or she can.

If in the past you have encouraged your employees to make decisions concerning their own work, what do they do now?

___**1.** They still come to me and want to share the responsibility for making the decision.

___**2.** A few of my employees make the decision first, then tell me later.

___**3.** Most of my employees make the minor decisions affecting their work without my approval.

___**4.** There are one or two employees I have to keep an eye on, because they tend to overstep their boundaries of decision-making.

___**5.** I still have one or two employees who would never make a decision that affected their work, even if their lives depended upon it.

___**6.** I still insist that all my employees check out with me all work decisions they make which affect their jobs, in the event something might go wrong.

If a group of your employees engaged in a job suddenly came upon a rather new problem which would affect them directly and immediately, what would they do?

___**1.** Stop all work and send a representative of the group to seek your help.

___**2.** Briefly discuss the problem, reach a solution, make a group decision, and continue working.

___**3.** Stop that phase of the job, seek your help, but continue to work on other aspects of the job until a decision was made by you.

___**4.** Stop doing everything and wait for you to come by and make a decision for the group.

___**5.** Seek the advice of the senior employee of the group, abide by his or her decision, and continue working on the job.

If one of your better employees made a decision on his or her own and it proved to be wrong and costly, and you were harshly reprimanded by your superior as a result of it, what would you do?

___**1.** Take the entire blame for permitting your subordinate to make the decision.

___**2.** Explain to your superior that this is your management style, that is, you encourage and permit your subordinates to make decisions that affect their work, and as a result your subordinate made an honest mistake.

___**3.** Chew out the subordinate who made the poor decision, and instruct him or her to check with you in the future on all decisions.

___**4.** Review the consequences of the decision with the subordinate, mutually examine his or her errors in judgment, but encourage the subordinate to continue making decisions.

___**5.** Call a meeting with all your subordinates and establish a new departmental policy, that everyone must check out every decision with you first, before making it.

___**6.** Call a meeting with all your subordinates, explain what happened, encourage them to continue their decision-making skills but to use more discretion. Then state that if they encounter some doubt they are to contact you.

Do you encourage your subordinates to participate actively in any of the following programs? (Encouragement is defined as giving them advice when asked, seeking their suggestions and ideas, or helping them execute their plans.)

___**1.** Taking part in company-sponsored suggestion programs.

___**2.** Developing improved methods concerning their job.

___**3.** Getting involved in outside community activities, such as Junior

Achievement, running for a political office, or scouting organizations.

___**4.** Assisting in accident prevention programs.

___**5.** Establishing departmental goals and objectives.

___**6.** Participating in post-high school education programs.

___**7.** Contributing to housekeeping improvement programs.

___**8.** Participating in various in-house control programs such as inventory control, or production/scheduling control programs.

___**9.** Helping make departmental policy changes (dress codes, or flex-scheduling).

Indicate how you think your subordinates would rate you in your role as:

1. A motivating manager

___(a) The best

___(b) Pretty good

___(c) Just fair

___(d) Poor

___(e) A real demotivator

2. A delegator manager

___(a) Delegates too much

___(b) Delegates pretty well

___(c) Just fair (my manager ducks the tough ones)

___(d) Poor (I have to get permission to go to the rest room!)

Recognition as a motivating force

Every normal human being has a need to be recognized. People want to belong, they want to be liked, they want to be appreciated, they want to be praised when they deserve praise, and they want to be respected by others so they can have a degree of self-respect. Tons of literature have been written about this subject, so I will not belabor the point any further.

The problem that exists with recognition as a motivating force for managers and supervisors is common. Recognition must start at the top of an organization and permeate downward through the various levels of management. Simply stated, if my superior doesn't give me some form of recognition occasionally (money excluded), how then can he expect me to give recognition to my employees? It's a matter of conditioning. For instance, if I am never praised, how can I be expected to praise those under me? But on the other hand, when I am praised, I respond favorably to it, and am more likely to praise others.

Praise and recognition make me feel good, and because I feel good and realize that my employees helped me receive this credit, it's much easier to extend this conditioned response to my employees. Why is this so? Because we're all human beings and we pretty much respond the same way to recognition, or lack of recognition, regardless of our rank or status within the organizational hierarchy. To view the process in another way, I've seen countless situations where a manager was "chewed out" by his superiors, left the confrontation, and immediately vented his anger and humiliation on the first employee he came across.

Whenever managers or supervisors are not given positive or favorable recognition over a long period of time, especially when they deserve it, they will tend to build defensive mechanisms toward others, including their employees and superiors. This is an unhealthy mental attitude to create among middle managers and lower-level supervisors, and its usefulness as a so-called management technique is questionable. For example, I once worked under a superior whose consistent comments to me and to other supervisors were always negative. It seemed the harder I and my employees tried, the more negative recognition we would receive. What did we do? Collectively, we were all demotivated. We simply quit trying so hard and did only our normal work load. Other supervisors and groups did the same. The more he fussed and fumed, the less attention we paid him.

There's absolutely no place for this type of management style in today's work world. Managers and their employees are too intelligent and socially aware to be treated without regard for their human dignity and their self-respect.

A MOTIVATIONAL INVENTORY FOR MEASURING RECOGNITION

How much recognition do you give each employee in your department? When do you give recognition, in what form, and how often?

The following questions have been developed to serve as a guide in evaluating your personal efforts when giving recognition to your individual employees. (In order for this inventory to be effective you must make an individual assessment for each employee.)

EMPLOYEE NAME _____

1. When was the last time you personally complimented this employee for something he or she had accomplished?

_____

2. Briefly describe the circumstances involved that merited your personal compliment.

_____

_____

3. What did you do or say when you complimented this employee?

I said the following:_____

I did the following: _____

4. If you have never complimented this employee, why not?

_____

_____

5. What is this employee's most outstanding quality?

_____

6. After you have properly identified this employee's most outstanding quality, give a brief example of how you have attempted to bring out this quality in a job situation or circumstance.

_____

_____

7. What is this employee's most important weakness when performing his or her job?

_____

_____

8. After you have properly identified this employee's most important weakness when performing his or her job, describe briefly what you have done to correct it.

_____

_____

9. When was the last time you personally asked this employee for his or her suggestions or advice?

---

10. What was the employee's response when you asked him or her for advice or suggestions?

---

11. What have you done in the past to make this employee important in your department? (Note: This question does not mean what have you done to make the employee *feel* important.)

---

12. What other things could you do to give additional recognition to this employee that you haven't done in the past?

Group motivational patterns and the natural leader

If managing consisted only of dealing with individuals and not groups, the job would be a snap. But unfortunately that is not the case and never has been. Man is by his nature a social animal. He is born into groups and lives, works, dies, and is buried within groups. There is no escape from group life.

It is no wonder, then, that managers who try to interfere too much with the informally structured work group soon find their task more difficult. Small work groups tend to exchange ideas when searching for motivational force and direction, as well as when seeking demotivational factors. Members of work groups determine their own values, production quotas, rewards, and punishments.

Motivating a work group requires different skills and techniques from motivating an individual. I have always found that the most successful way to motivate a work group is to win over the support of the natural leader. By doing this you can bring into play techniques and skills used to motivate an individual, and still affect the total group. The following suggests techniques aimed at motivating natural leaders and thus their group members.

AN INVENTORY FOR MEASURING MOTIVATIONAL PATTERNS

How familiar are you with the various motivational patterns that exist within groups of employees you manage? Read and answer each question below in order to gain insight into successful motivational techniques you might consider using when managing your group of employees.

1. Are you familiar with the term "natural leader"?___Yes ___No (If you're not sure, review Chapter 1 in this book.)

2. Can you identify by name the natural leader(s) in your work group? ___Yes ___No

3. If yes, who are they?

_____

_____

4. What qualities tend to make those individuals natural leaders?

_____   _____   _____

5. At the present time, how would you rate the relationship of the natural leader(s) to yourself?
___Very cooperative   ___Somewhat cooperative
___Mostly neutral   ___Somewhat unfriendly
___Very unfriendly

6. What degree of authority and responsibility do you permit your natural leader(s) to exercise?
___Complete authority and responsibility for all assignments
___Limited authority and responsibility
___Very little authority and responsibility
___Absolutely no authority and responsibility

7. How often do you seek the advice and/or suggestions of your natural leader(s)?
___Quite frequently (almost daily)
___Sometimes (once a week)
___Very little (once a month)
___Hardly ever

8. If you were absent from work because of vacation or illness, would you permit the natural leader to take over your position? ___Yes ___No ___Someone other than the natural leader is already assigned that function

9. At the present time, how effective is the natural leader in controlling the production of your group?

___Too effective to suit me

___Very effective at times

___Somewhat effective

___Very ineffective

10. At the present time do you feel that the work goals of the natural leader are:

___About the same as mine

___Totally different from mine

___Sometimes the same and sometimes different

11. Do you ever make "political deals" with natural leaders to get their cooperation, or to "pay them off" for accomplishing unpleasant work tasks? (Such payoffs might be preferential vacation time, special favors, and/or socializing off the job.)

___Sometimes yes   ___Occasionally I might

___Absolutely not

12. Do you make note of the informal social groups that organize themselves within your department? (For instance, who eats together, what individuals commute together, or who participates in outside activities together?)

___Yes   ___No

13. If you answered Yes to question 12, have you ever utilized these informal organized social groups to accomplish the following:

___Solve a difficult work problem

___Meet a critical deadline

___Increase and maintain productivity

___Obtain their group opinions about organizational policy

___Obtain their group suggestions when taking on a new procedure or new product

14. Do you encourage informal social group activities during working hours such as "flower funds," or playing cards at lunch time?

___Yes, all the time   ___Sometimes I do

___Very rarely   ___Never

15. Do you participate in informal social group activities during working hours such as "flower funds," or playing cards at lunch time?

___Yes, all the time   ___Sometimes I do

___Very rarely   ___Never

16. Do you find it easier to motivate an individual employee than a group of employees?
___Both are about the same
___The individual is easier to motivate
___The group is easier to motivate

Money as a motivator

If you ask a group of people how many of them think they deserve a raise, almost all will raise their hands. Of course, this is a natural reaction, because only a fool would turn down a raise. If you then ask how many think they are being paid what they are worth, a few may raise their hands, but the majority of the group will not. If you then ask how many think they are underpaid for the responsibilities they have, about half will raise their hands. Finally, if you ask how many think they are being overpaid in their present job, I can guarantee that very few people will respond affirmatively.

Is money, in the form of wages, salaries, bonuses, piece work, and incentive payments, a *real* motivator, or is it used by management as a manipulator? Its value in our contemporary work world is conditioned by its importance to each recipient. With the present high cost of living and double-digit inflation, money means more to more people than at any time in the past. There are some interesting aspects of money that the reader must be aware of before trying to answer the question.

Money as a benchmark. The wages and/or salary one receives often serves as a measuring instrument by its recipients because of the universality of the meaning of money. What one can do with money, as well as the amount one receives, serves as a means of comparing one's worth against others within the same work group, or in other organizations.

Job titles and money. Job titles and the accompanying salary one receives are at times misleading. For instance, a vice president with a masters degree in business administration, working in a financial institution, may receive the same as or even less than the weekly garbage collector who may have been a high school dropout. Is money a real motivator in this case? For the vice president, the answer is probably no, but for the garbage collector, it could be yes.

Money as a lure. If money isn't a motivator, why then do so many organizations lose excellent employees who were lured away by higher financial rewards? This includes executive secretaries, non-degreed highly skilled technicians, plant managers, and even corporate presidents.

Money as a symbol. Wages and salaries can act as a symbol when combined with other satisfying job or work factors, such as hours required to work, working conditions, responsibilities, the amount of decision-making required, and the dangers and hazards involved in performing work. Obviously, the relationship between the effort one must put forth and the monetary gain received must also be considered.

Money as a group cohesive. There have been very few times that I have seen money serve as a true motivator. On one occasion, while working as a supervisor in an open hearth department of a steel mill I observed four first helpers exercise group solidarity to achieve maximum incentive earnings. (A first helper is one who is totally responsible for making x number of tons of molten steel at about 2,800 degrees Fahrenheit.) This was a continuous operation, seven days a week, around the clock. The four individuals worked different shifts, but were assigned to one furnace to produce the steel. Most of these men had not graduated from high school, but they could figure their incentive earnings almost to the penny. Even though each man worked individually on his own respective shift, they collectively combined their skills and hard work into a team effort to take advantage of the incentive system established by the industrial engineering department.

On the other hand, I witnessed a somewhat different approach to incentive earnings. At one time in my career, I served for a very short period of time as a safety director in a foundry. Management and the union mutually agreed that if the work crews could produce in five hours what it normally took to do in eight hours, the men could go home early and would be paid the same rate, plus incentive. Needless to say, management got what it wanted, and the employees got what they wanted. But it cost both parties, because safety was thrown to the winds, and there were several severe burn cases, cuts, and broken bones. The organization was cited and fined many times by government inspectors from the Occupational Safety and Health Administration.

Money as a prize. When money is the main prize in a sales contest, the contestants will inevitably ask themselves what the probability is of winning the contest. Many variables, such as number and size of clients, the national economic picture, the same product mix versus a different product mix, the price of the product in relation to net profit, and the number of contestants, will have a direct bearing on an individual's probablility of winning.

Whether an employee decides to enter the contest depends on the amount of the monetary award compared to the base salary. If for instance, one contestant earns $30,000 per year, and the top prize is $1,000, there is little incentive. But another contestant, who earns $10,000 per year base salary, may readily accept the challenge and be spurred on to try and win.

The amount of effort needed to win the contest also affects the decision to compete. If it means extremely long hours and extra days of work, some contestants may or may not be willing to accept the challenge.

Conclusion. Money means different things to different people in different work organizations and at different times in their work careers. Likewise, money means different things to different managements in different businesses and industries, and at different times in the history and life of these organizations. Therefore, when these three major forces are brought together—people, organizations, and money—*the question of money as a motivator or manipulator is determined by how well it serves both the individual and the organization.* How the individual and the organization wish to perceive money (manipulative versus motivational) is a matter of personal choice in a free capitalistic society. Today, however, one must never forget the influence of both national and worldwide economic policies and practices.

9 PERFORMANCE APPRAISALS

The Managerial Ratings Game

Employee growth and development is, in the final sense, self-development. Over an extended period of time, or even an entire work career, employees write their own tickets for advancement. But all of us need guidance along the way to arrive at a genuine meeting of minds between superiors and subordinates. This can be accomplished through performance appraisal techniques.

On the other hand, there are those who say that a manager should never have to resort to the use of annual reviews, performance reviews, or performance appraisals. They contend that this business of managing people should involve constant, almost daily face-to-face feedback regarding subordinates' quality of performance. If we as managers want to bring about behavior changes and improve the work performance of our subordinates, we can only do so when there is frequent feedback about the work behavior.

Why, then, do we have performance appraisals? What are the dangers and pitfalls of performance appraisals, and what successful performance appraisal techniques might managers use to accomplish their purposes? These questions will be answered in this chapter.

Why performance appraisals?

Work performance appraisals provide managers and management with the following:

1. A measure of control over work activities and subordinates.
2. An objective measure for establishing salary levels and determining eligibility for promotions.
3. Better utilization of existing manpower, as well as an inventory of human resources talent within an organization.
4. The means to improve subordinate performance on the job through managerial guidance.
5. Formalized, periodic feedback to let employees know how they are doing in the eyes of their managers.
6. An incentive for employees to improve.
7. A means to focus managers' attention on their main concern, namely, the subordinates they manage.
8. Meaningful interaction between a manager and subordinate, and one in which both parties can learn additional information about each other, as well as about the job in question.
9. Valuable information when developing preemployment tests and test validation.
10. A source of information for developing future training and development programs for nonmanagement as well as management personnel.
11. An indication of the effectiveness of the managers themselves.
12. A means to motivate subordinates to examine their own work objectively with a view to changing those habits and attitudes that are considered ineffective or disruptive in the workplace.
13. Documentary evidence that may be needed to terminate the consistently poor performer who is beyond being salvaged.

The dangers and pitfalls of performance appraisals

Of the many dangers and pitfalls involved in making performance appraisals, I shall describe only those that seem to be the most frequently mentioned by both subordinates and managers.

1. Many managers, adhering to the old adage, "Judge not and ye shall not be judged," are reluctant to undertake performance appraisals. They therefore have a tendency to lean toward an overly positive attitude, thus hindering objectivity. Other stumbling blocks to objectivity are a manager's personal bias and the difficulty of assigning proper weight to various job factors being evaluated.

2. Because performance appraisals are conducted only once or twice a year at best, managers often lack a complete grasp of the criteria necessary to make a truly objective evaluation of their subordinates' work performance. They become rusty at the process, and find they must review the performance appraisal procedure manual to conduct this exercise, which may have been forced upon them by the personnel department.

3. The total time a manager spends with a subordinate on an annual or semiannual performance appraisal is insufficient to bring about effective changes in work habits or attitudes. For instance, let's assume an employee works 50 weeks a year at a rate of 40 hours per week. This comes to 2,000 work hours per year, so that a one-hour appraisal is actually 1/2,000th of the total employee's time. Even two appraisals per year, each one hour long, bring the fraction of time spent to 2/2,000, or 1/1,000th of the total employee's time. Pretty slim odds in either case—when you're trying to change behavior or improve subordinates' productivity! Furthermore, imagine if you can, how much employee growth and development can be accomplished in one or two hours per year.

4. When managers emphasize an employee's deficiencies or weaknesses too much during the performance appraisal, they can unknowingly intensify the subordinate's anxieties. Thus the manager is viewed as a threat, and can no longer be perceived as a resource individual by the employee. When this occurs, and subordinates feel a lack of encouragement from their managers, performance failure is guaranteed. If the employee being evaluated becomes too preoccupied with what the manager perceives as weaknesses or shortcomings, the entire performance appraisal session may turn into a highly negative situation that can prove distasteful to both parties.

5. It has always been assumed that the manager is totally qualified to review a subordinate's performance, and by the same token,

the subordinate believes his or her manager is eminently qualified. This means that the manager should have a thorough understanding of the subordinate's job functions as well as the relation of the job to his or her own department. Unfortunately, this is not the case. Job content changes too rapidly in our contemporary work world.

6. Often managers cannot distinguish the differences in roles they must play during the entire performance appraisal process. To be effective, a manager must take on the role of a judge, as well as the role of a counselor or coach. Too many managers, however, perceive these as conflicting roles and thus nullify their own integrity in the eyes of the appraisee.

7. There's a vast difference between the qualifications a manager needs to *review* a subordinate's performance, and the qualifications needed to *evaluate* performance. By the very nature of this superior-subordinate interaction process, managers are hard pressed to completely divorce themselves from being subjective in either the *review* or *evaluation* functions of performance appraisals.

8. A performance appraisal is essentially an interview in which friendly conversation must take place, so that both parties can exchange ideas and benefit from the process. However, when the manager has not been properly trained in the skills of conducting an interview, or the subordinate refrains from entering into the conversation, the anticipated benefits cannot be obtained.

9. One must always consider the manager who is not trusted by his or her subordinates, as well as the insecure manager, and the effects their presentation of the performance appraisal will have upon their subordinates. The appraisal interview implies an openness, leveling, and mutual trust between superior and subordinate. However, if subordinates distrust their managers, or perceive their managers as insecure, the effectiveness of the appraisal is in great jeopardy.

10. When writing performance appraisals it is rather easy to develop and measure quantitative criteria and standards. Such quantitative criteria are units of production, accident frequencies, volume of sales dollars, methods improvements, and cost reductions. However, in the less tangible areas of subordinates' work, the attempt to reduce

judgmental criteria or qualitative criteria to writing is much more difficult. Ability to communicate, initiative, degree of cooperativeness, and ability to get along with others are but a few examples of qualitative criteria.

11. Too many managers cannot separate personality appraisals from performance appraisals. Some managers have a tendency to become entangled in personal traits rather than actual performance traits. When this happens, the appraisal becomes unreliable, leads to generalities, meaningless comparisons, and useless counseling.

12. Formal performance appraisals are a poor substitute for the informal day-to-day appraisals and conversations that should transpire between managers and their employees. Transferring the performance review to a sterile, well-còntrolled environment, on a periodic basis, is sometimes such a good, even if inadvertent, camouflage that some subordinates fail to realize that they have been appraised.

13. Most organizations require managers to complete performance appraisal forms for each of the employees under them. Even though employees are encouraged to express their opinions about their managers' evaluations, many view their roles as passive. Whenever mutual involvement is not encouraged by the manager, the performance appraisal process becomes a one-way communication process with little being accomplished by both parties.

14. Too much emphasis is placed on the performance appraisal form and its administration. Many managers want to do things right by adhering strictly to policy and procedures as defined in the performance appraisal manual, rather than concentrating on the interaction process with their subordinates, especially in the areas of employee growth and development, as well as potential contributions to the organization.

15. Performance appraisals try to achieve too many objectives within a single program—salary increases, developing human talent, improving individual performance, judging on the one hand and counseling on the other, and motivating employees, to mention a few. Moreover, the timing of the appraisal and the ritualistic ceremonial views conveyed to many subordinates can make all these worthwhile objectives totally incompatible.

16. Because there is a wide variety and range of jobs, who in the organization decides which job traits or characteristics are going to be rated? Furthermore, can there be an agreement on a definition of each job trait or characteristic? And finally, should all job traits or characteristics have the same relative value for all employees within the same organization?

17. The importance of timing cannot be overlooked in the performance appraisal process. Since most reviews are on an annual or semiannual basis, the goals an employee works toward seldom have an exact 12-month or 6-month corresponding deadline. To formally appraise an employee months after a project has been successfully completed causes a manager to lose much of the psychological impact of an appraisal made at the time of the completion of the project.

18. Finally, when formal training is abandoned for both the appraiser and the appraisee, when purposes and values for administering and conducting performance appraisals are not thoroughly defined and explained, and when slipshod methods are used by managers in a hurry to complete what many consider a distasteful task, the end result is a total farce, and the entire program should be scrapped!

Performance appraisal interviewing techniques

One must keep in mind there are several phases to the performance appraisal process, for instance, the appraisal of an employee, which is normally made in the absence of the employee, and the post-performance appraisal interview, which is conducted in the presence of the employee. It is the latter phase, the interview, that we shall discuss in this section.

PREPARATION

To prepare for the postperformance appraisal interview, or discussion, managers should select a time and place that will provide as few interruptions as possible. Review each individual's form thoroughly before the discussion interview starts. You may want to check off certain key points to discuss with each employee before the beginning of the interview.

BEGINNING THE INTERVIEW

When individuals present themselves, make them comfortable and at ease. Always tell the employee that this is a review, or performance appraisal, or whatever name your organization calls it. It makes sense to quickly review the objectives and procedures of the program with each individual. Emphasize the basic purpose of the program, which is normally to help individuals improve their work performance. The situation is eased if you say that no one is perfect, including yourself. Tell the individual that you want and expect him or her to ask questions, make comments, and participate in a wide open discussion. After these brief comments, don't beat around the bush—get right down to business.

Whether or not you discuss the actual ratings or show the individual the performance appraisal form is a procedural matter that has been established by your organization. (This point will be discussed in the following section of this chapter.) I like to start the discussion by talking about an individual's strong points, and refer to specific examples or jobs that have been done well. This again is a personal choice, but I feel it puts both parties at ease, and breaks the ice.

SELF-EVALUATION AS A TECHNIQUE FOR
DISCUSSING DEFICIENCIES

One successful technique that managers can use to introduce the subject of deficiencies or weaknesses is to ask individuals where they think they could improve. The strategy at this point is to get the employees to open up and possibly identify an area that they perceive to be suboptimal. If the individual fails to point out an area that you perceive as a deficiency, then obviously you must present the subject. This point can be very difficult, and may well make or break the entire discussion. First, *identify* the specific area, such as quality or quantity of work that you wish to discuss.

Second, point out to the individual that any comments you are about to make are to be considered as *constructive criticism* and represent only your point of view. Third, pinpoint a specific example or examples, and be prepared to present facts. It is most important that facts are revealed, not hearsay or opinions. Remember also that the area of weakness should always be of sufficient impact or consequence to the job itself.

THE MANAGER AS A RESOURCE PERSON

Assuming the individual accepts your comments as constructive and doesn't get emotionally upset, and, more particularly, agrees with your comments, you may want to explore in greater detail any problems or misunderstandings he or she may have concerning this specific task. Here you may realize that part of the individual's weakness may have been your fault, or that additional training is needed. The next point separates the mature manager from the immature manager: Offer to aid or help the individual in the future. Too many managers give glib guidance and pompous suggestions instead of concrete aid. Your role in this most important interaction process is to be a resource individual to each and every one of your subordinates. Employees today can spot phoniness, insecurity, and hollow rhetoric, especially during a performance appraisal interview.

Begin being a resource person by meeting briefly and informally with the subordinate in question on a regular basis (daily or weekly). Here you discuss the progress of an assignment or make suggestions based on your experience. Many times a manager can directly contact another manager and ask for help or suggestions that will open doors and expedite the solution to the problem. This makes it easier for the subordinate to gain additional information, and still prevents you from doing the actual work. Suggest reference books, magazine articles, or past research projects that the person can consult. This approach will force the subordinate to dig for additional data and will also broaden his or her background and knowledge about the assignment. If appropriate, visits to the problem work area with your subordinate can be helpful—on-site activities permit critical observations, comparisons, and helpful discussions concerning the assigned project.

DISCUSSION TECHNIQUES

Basically, a performance appraisal interview should be a conversation between two people. It is the manager's responsibility to try to maintain a tone of friendliness during the entire procedure and to keep the discussion moving along. There are two discussion techniques a successful manager can use: the direct and the indirect. When managers use the direct discussion method, they guide the dialogue through key questions or statements. When using the indirect discussion method, the manager encourages the employee to move the dialogue along by permitting the individual to do most of the talking—either by asking questions or making statements.

Managers who have developed the skill of indirect discussion methods find it more advantageous because employees take an active part in the dialogue and raise critical points that concern them. This is what you want to do, because it will help you better understand your employees' attitude toward the job and the various tasks involved in it. In this atmosphere of understanding, employees can begin to recognize their own strengths or weaknesses and can criticize their own work performance without damaging their self-esteem. Furthermore, this technique makes employees more receptive to advice and help because it is much easier to accept self-criticism than to accept criticism from someone else, especially one's superior. Once employees understand the need to improve some aspect of their work behavior, they have sold themselves on the principles of self-recognition of a problem and self-acceptance of trying to correct it.

PARAPHRASING AS A TECHNIQUE

Another technique that managers can use in conjunction with the indirect discussion method is to paraphrase, or repeat the employee's critical statements. In order to do this, the manager must listen closely to what is said, then repeat in the form of an indirect question what the employee has just said. For instance, the employee may say, "I have a tough time getting all the information together for the month-end report." The manager, sensing this to be a critical point and a weakness, and realizing there is more to the statement than meets the ears, may say something like this, "Do I understand you correctly, when you say you have a tough time getting all the information you need for the month-end report?"

Now the employee knows that you know what the specific problem is, and meanwhile has had time to think over the next statement. Satisfied that you recognize the problem, because you've repeated it back, the employee really opens up and goes into detail about the problem. Even an occasional "hm-m-m" from the manager during the employee's discussion can bring forth additional comments that otherwise might never emerge.

TECHNIQUES FOR HANDLING DISAGREEMENTS

When a manager and an employee don't agree on a specific point, there are certain techniques managers must learn to use if they desire to conduct a successful performance appraisal. First, don't treat the disagreement as a major threat to your power, position, or authority. Instead, through the use of probing questions seek a clearer definition of what constitutes the disagreement. An employee may perceive you as making a false accusation about his or her performance and be ready to challenge your judgment. Don't be trapped into defending your position immediately. Back off gracefully, don't apologize, but continue to probe. Perhaps it was a certain word you used, or the inflection of your voice that aroused the employee's sense of pride. Many times it's simply a matter of degree as to how you both perceive a situation or circumstance.

If employees think they have done a satisfactory job, and you feel just the opposite, and say so, they will not criticize their own work, because they don't think and feel they have done poorly. Thus you put the employee on the defensive and remove the probability of self-analysis and self-criticism. Your goal as a manager should be to find a basis of agreement between yourself and the employee that accurately reflects the employee's performance. At the same time, any misunderstandings should be cleared up so that together you both can develop mutually agreeable goals for the future.

DIFFERENT STROKES FOR DIFFERENT FOLKS

Intelligent managers will always tailor their approach to the specific employee they are interviewing. Again, permit me to emphasize one of the cardinal principles of successful management: you must get to know your employees. You must know what their social tolerances are, their attitudes toward you, the job, the organization; what is most important is how you communicate and what types of comments you can make to them, especially during the performance appraisal interview. Before deciding on the approach you will use, ask yourself these questions:

1. How well do I really know this individual?
2. How candid can I be with this individual when discussing his or her deficiencies?
3. Am I thoroughly prepared to point out specific examples of strengths and weaknesses?
4. If I have corrected this individual in the past, what have been his or her reactions?
5. How well does the individual accept praise?
6. How well does the individual accept constructive criticism?
7. If I have reviewed this individual's past performance, what were some of the critical areas we discussed? Has there been improvement in these areas?
8. Does the individual like to participate in setting his or her own goals?
9. Does the employee prefer to have me set his or her goals?
10. What specific jobs has he or she been concentrating on since the last review?
11. Does the type of work permit any latitude in goal setting? If so, how much?
12. Have there been any major changes in this individual's personal life, such as marriage, divorce, births, or deaths of family members, illnesses, and so forth, that could affect his or her work performance?

I am sure the answers to these questions will guide you in tailoring the most effective approach to the performance appraisal interview.

HERE COMES THE JUDGE

One of the least effective techniques is to overplay your role as a manager by acting as a judge. I would imagine that 99 percent of all performance appraisal interviews are conducted by managers sitting behind their desks, or on one side of a conference table, with the subordinate sitting in front of the desk, or on the opposite side of the table. The desk or table becomes a psychological barrier, as well as an

actual one, as so often occurs during labor contract negotiations between management and union representatives. Get out from behind
your desk (the judge's bench in this case), and sit beside your subordinate, thus removing this psychological barrier. Try it—it will make
a difference!

Another way to prevent acting like a judge is to avoid merely
telling your subordinates their strengths and weaknesses and denying
them the opportunity for discussion. For the employee, this is like
listening to the judge hand down a sentence in the courtroom. Furthermore, this technique is too academic and demotivating to your
subordinates.

COACHING AS OPPOSED TO JUDGING

One of the more successful techniques is to conduct yourself like a
coach, rather than a judge. In this case you don't have to reveal your
evaluations of subordinates' performance. Instead, mention the items
to be appraised and encourage employees to appraise their own performance. When they acknowledge weaknesses, you suggest ways
they can set their own goals, with the assurance that you will help
them try to achieve these goals. Or you may suggest alternatives
that they may use to reach these goals. This technique is more likely
to help employees retain their dignity and self-respect, which is so
critical in our contemporary work world.

Furthermore, this technique will often reveal to both parties that
employees did not know what was expected of them in relation to
their jobs. It may also reveal that the employees didn't know how to
do what was expected, or for some reason couldn't do the job. This
may pinpoint the need for additional training and/or on-the-job instruction. It may also point out unequal work loads, or the need to
transfer employees to more suitable work, or even to change or
reorganize the employees' work routine to better utilize their
strengths. Finally, it may also indicate that now is the time to
seriously consider getting rid of a poor performer.

SUMMARIZE THE PERFORMANCE APPRAISAL INTERVIEW

At the close of the performance appraisal interview successful
managers will briefly summarize the employees' strengths and/or

areas where they can improve. Make a commitment to help the employee who needs help. At this point many marginal employees have been salvaged and completely turned around because of a sincere commitment and follow-up by their managers. Too many employees limp away from a performance appraisal interview totally confused, frustrated, and demotivated, because they feel they have been sentenced by "the judge." They remain confused for weeks and months, not knowing what they are expected to do, and yet wanting to do what is expected of them. So what started out to be a fine management development tool ends up as a demoralizing, demotivating, and degrading disaster.

Performance appraisal techniques

This section of the chapter deals with 11 different performance appraisal techniques, or ways to evaluate employee job performance. Usually organizations determine which method or technique to use on the basis of the number and types of employees to be evaluated (management, salaried, and union-eligible), the types of functions the employees perform, available time to carry out evaluations, the amount of time available to train evaluators, available funds, and most important, the use of the results of the evaluation.

CHECKLISTS

Checklists, one of the oldest and most popular techniques in use today, attempt to define behavior or traits that apply to a job the individual is doing. The appraisal form usually consists of a list of performance criteria for doing certain jobs and provides a rating scale for evaluating the individual's job performance. The drawback is that the checklist is designed for use in evaluating all kinds of employees who are performing a variety of jobs. Thus it is *not* the best evaluation form to use, because the performance criteria for one type of job may not be applicable when measuring performance of a different task.

THE RANKING METHOD

The ranking method compares the relative performance of one member of a small work group with all other members of the same group. This technique can be used by a manager to rank employees' overall performance or specific parts of their performance. Essentially, this comparison type of evaluation is designed for small work groups of 5 to 10 individuals. The results are applicable only to the group being evaluated. There are basically three ways of making such ranking methods: rank order, paired comparisons, and forced distribution.

In the rank-order method, the manager simply ranks a group of employees from best to poorest, on part or all of the job, by arranging a set of name cards or the employees' appraisal forms.

Whenever managers want to make direct comparisons of employees, they can use the paired comparisons technique. The manager makes up a series of 3×5 index cards. Each card carries the names of two employees, so that each employee is rated against every other employee in the work group. The manager compares the two names on each card, and marks or checks the name of the employee he or she considers higher on performance. After all the cards have been reviewed in this manner, the manager goes back through the entire series of cards and tabulates the total number of times each name has been checked. The name with the most checkmarks ranks highest; the name with the fewest checkmarks ranks lowest; and those names between the highest and lowest are ranked in order of the number of checkmarks received.

There are several obvious drawbacks to this technique. It is too time-consuming to use on large numbers of employees, and managers' biases can enter in too easily. Also, it is difficult to properly measure more than one criterion at a time using this technique.

The forced distribution technique forces managers to place all their employees into predetermined percentages of distribution, much like a bell-shaped curve. Thus, 5 percent of the employees must be ranked superior, 10 percent above average, 70 percent average, 10 percent below average, and 5 percent poor. The manager judges each employee on the basis of the appraisal form he or she is using, and then places the employees' names into one of these five categories. If the percentage distribution does not match the predetermined pattern, the manager must rework the forms until they do, or settle for a skewed bell-shaped curve distribution.

This technique might well be used when a mandatory cutback of nonunion employees is required and the manager is forced to reduce work crews. The fact that managers are forced to distribute their employees along a continuum leaves much to be desired in terms of the factors used to evaluate each employee.

JOB DESCRIPTIONS AS A BASIS FOR APPRAISALS

Some organizations believe that performance appraisal forms should be developed along the lines of the individual's job description. In this manner a manager can compare the individual's job performance over a period of time against the requirements spelled out in the job description. Theoretically this technique appears to offer many advantages, such as collecting specific examples of an employee's performance, so that a more accurate evaluation can be made. It is also suggested that during the appraisal interview managers can use the forms as documented evidence to support their evaluations. Such documentation will also help employees to improve performance, where needed, by showing them in specific, tangible terms where their deficiencies lie.

This technique appears to provide a solid basis for evaluating employee performance, but it is inadequate for two reasons. First, it is assumed that the manager has a close working knowledge of each individual's job description, and that the job description is up to date. Second, a constant monitoring of employees' work behavior must be made almost daily and the observations recorded for each individual so that solid, factual examples of job performance can be presented during the appraisal interview. But in practice, the technique makes no allowances for managers' absences from the workplace. Nor does it make allowances for managers whose busy schedules do not permit them to constantly document outstanding as well as deficient job performance.

THE PLAN, WORK, REVIEW TECHNIQUE

Some organizations have adopted a plan, work, review technique to motivate performance improvement in employees. Unfortunately, the application of this technique has only been at the professional and administrative middle management level, and has not permeated downward to the lower levels in the hierarchy. In essence the technique is quite simple, because it creates a continuous interaction in which managers and subordinates frequently plan and discuss performance prior to, during, and after completion of a work project. The main emphasis is on mutual goal setting, planning, and mutual problem solving. It is felt that subordinate performance improves because specific goals are established. Where mutual goal setting is involved and subordinates contribute toward it, they acquire ownership of part of the decision-making process that takes place, and as a result are not going to permit the project to fail. Because of this, subordinates' efforts and performance improve. Finally, it is thought that daily coaching on the part of the manager contributes more to improving employee performance than the traditional annual or semiannual reviews.

Unfortunately, this technique is seldom used with lower levels of employees in organizations. Over the years, contemporary management has conditioned the base level of union-eligible employees to accept the "horse race," insidious, industrial engineering methods of more and more production at the expense of better human relations. Life in the front-line trenches—the production line—is totally different from life at the administrative and professional levels. I know, because I have lived and worked in both areas.

THE PARTICIPATIVE MANAGEMENT TECHNIQUE

To establish standards of performance for managers' positions does not mean to "standardize" them, but rather to tell managers how well they should do it. The greatest need for more precise standards of job performance in managerial positions is in the direction of their subordinates. All managers need a yardstick with which to determine how effectively they are applying the basic principles of management.

A technique for setting standards of performance for managers is participative management, which calls for executives to work out standards of performance appraisal with the help and participation of their subordinate managers. To do this executives should collaborate with those managers who have similar jobs. Managers who are permitted to participate in such a group approach will more readily accept these performance standards simply because they helped to establish them.

The participative management technique requires the entire group, including the executive, to determine what each job factor is, before determining how well that factor should be done. In this manner the entire group gains more understanding and cooperation as a result of sharing, identifying, and describing what each manager does in his or her job. The most difficult part is to define in specific, yet objective language, the elements of a particular job function. Furthermore, standards should not be set too high, so that realistic performance can be attained in light of current operating circumstances. Once managerial performance standards are established, the subordinate managers will have precise goals at which to aim, and because of ownership of these goals, through the participative management technique, they will exert greater effort to fulfill them.

THE MANAGER'S MONTHLY LETTER

While serving as a training specialist at corporate headquarters of the GTI Corporation in Pittsburgh, Pennsylvania, I was privy to the various plant managers' monthly letters sent to the president. This technique was an extension of a systematic managerial performance budgeting program developed by top-level management. Generally, it worked as follows:

At the end of each month, each plant manager was to write a manager's letter and have it on the president's desk by the 15th day of the following month. Preparation of the monthly objectives, or performance budgets, was the sole responsibility of each plant manager. Fulfillment of the performance budget, however, was the responsibility of the plant manager and his management team.

It was apparent that the president was searching for positive results at the end of each month, assuming, of course, that the plant manager and his team carried out their duties and performed as anticipated. Likewise, each plant manager and his team of managers would be accountable for the results they obtained at the conclusion of each month. It was also incumbent upon each plant manager to briefly anticipate the forthcoming month's performance budgets and report these in the same manager's letter.

What made the system effective was the fact that each plant manager and his team of managers established standards for themselves. Thus, mature managerial appraisal and development was being achieved because the effort to establish performance budgets and maintain managerial improvement originated with the plant manager and his team of managers, instead of being mandated through top-level planning and direction from the president.

THE ASSESSMENT CENTER TECHNIQUE

When appraising potentials in employees, managers should turn their attention to the assessment center technique, a relatively new technique for identifying and developing management and sales potential in your organization. Assessment centers differ from other identification and selection techniques in that a number of employees are assessed at the same time by trained line managers who conduct the assessment centers using multiple business-simulated exercises to evaluate behavior. In a number of well-controlled studies, assessment centers have proved to be more accurate than the usual supervisory ratings and tests.

The outstanding advantages of this technique are flexibility and positive and early identification of those possessing management potential. A tremendous development and training tool, it teaches the assessor how to spot and develop dimensions of required management behavior in his subordinates as well as himself. The methods used in assessing individuals are job-related and simulate typical management situations and conditions. These are more representative and indicative of expected and anticipated managerial behavior than are paper-pencil tests, inventories, and interviews used by themselves.

The assessment center technique was originally developed by Douglas W. Bray, American Telephone and Telegraph's director of personnel research. Today, there are many excellent consulting firms which provide assessment center training programs. For instance, the American Management Associations in New York City conducts this type of training for organizations all over the country. Assessment centers are relatively inexpensive in terms of the long-range payoff, and can be developed and used by large, medium, and small companies that need to obtain objective analyses of their employee talents and potential.

TRAIT APPRAISAL AS A TECHNIQUE

This technique is the simplest and perhaps one of the most commonly used methods of performance appraisal. Basically, the manager follows a form which lists a series of traits, such as attitude, accuracy, appearance, etc. Usually the traits appraisal form includes sections dealing with performance traits, technical characteristics, and a space for comments and recommendations.

One advantage of this technique is that by using a standardized form, the management of an organization is assured some degree of uniformity among the various appraisers. However, this technique has some serious problems. The first is the problem of communication between managers and their subordinates, particularly when constructive criticism is necessary. Second, when an extended period of time has elapsed between appraisals, there is a natural tendency for the manager to remember only recent incidents, whether good or bad. Finally, the trait appraisal technique is a unilateral action because employees are never given a set of standards against which they can be measured. Obviously, by not actively involving employees, you prohibit them from participating in the establishment of goals and levels of performance that they may be able to achieve.

THE CRITICAL INCIDENT APPROACH

The critical incident approach is an effort to compensate for remembering only current or recent performance. Most critical incident forms are concerned with the appraisal of two major categories: work habits and personal characteristics. One major advantage of this technique is the significance of a manager's interacting and dealing with subordinates on a more regular and frequent basis. However, the employee is not required to participate actively in the appraisal reviews conducted by the manager. Furthermore, there is no assurance that subordinates have a sufficient understanding of what is expected from them in terms of levels of performance.

APPRAISAL BY RESULTS

The appraisal-by-results technique is based on employee participation in establishing goals against which performance is measured.
This technique is applicable at both the management and nonmanagement levels. Three basic steps are required to make it effective:

1. *The development of work descriptions.* Work descriptions are
not necessarily the same as job descriptions. The main difference is
that the employees express in their own words the scope and responsibilities of the job as they perceive it.

2. *Establishment of goals and accountability.* Employees and
their managers mutually establish goals that are attainable, measur-
able, and realistic. Goals must be attainable in order to prevent frustration during the forthcoming performance period. Goals must also
be capable of being objectively measured so that feedback assures
continuing effort. Finally, goals must be realistic in order to prevent
defeatism at the onset of the work period. These three factors when
combined make up the degree of accountability during the appraisal
interview.

3. *Performance feedback.* Constant feedback through communications with the manager assures the employee an opportunity
to measure performance prior to the appraisal interview. In a true
sense, the manager and subordinate are patterns in the business of
improving performance.

There are several advantages to using this technique. First, employees know during any period of performance what criteria they are
being measured against. Thus the employee is actively, rather than
passively, involved when striving to reach mutually predetermined
goals. Another advantage is the absence of special rating forms, since
there is no need for structured forms. Finally, the manager's role is
one of counselor, coach, and adviser to his or her subordinates. This
creates higher frequencies of interaction between managers and subordinates when helping employees achieve their objectives. If, in the
event, significant internal or external changes force the realignment
of goals, this technique is quite flexible and permits easy adaptability
to meet these changes.

THE SELF-APPRAISAL TECHNIQUE

In this technique, the subordinates are required to rate themselves on various factors, and then during the appraisal interview, they compare their self-evaluations to the evaluations by their managers. The advantage of using this technique includes a sharing of attitudes between superior and subordinate because of mutual and personal involvement during the interview. Subordinates no longer assume a passive role during the appraisal interview. It is felt that all parties learn more about themselves, their interacting relationships, their responsibilities to each other, and the importance and value of their jobs. Further, managers can learn more about factors which contribute to the difficulties their employees face on the job.

Some managers have indicated to me that one of the reasons they like this technique is the fact that they no longer had to "play God," or absorb the total impact and responsibility of evaluation. However, one of the major negative aspects of this technique is the inability or unwillingness of either party to successfully negotiate and reconcile *extreme* differences between their perceived ratings. For instance, if subordinates perceive themselves as performing excellently in the area of responsibility, but their managers evaluate the same factors as average, both parties must defend their evaluations. This might cause antagonism between the two parties which is carried through the balance of the appraisal interview.

# POWER AND POLITICS

Managers' Inseparable Twins

Power and politics are managers' inseparable twins, for one cannot survive without the other. Today's managers must learn three important aspects about power and politics if they hope to survive and to be successful in the future. They must (1) learn about the ramifications of power and politics, (2) learn how to acquire power through the use of political techniques, and (3) learn how to use power and political techniques effectively in their career.

The ramifications of power and politics

The ramifications of power are sometimes so well hidden in work organizations that subordinates are not aware that they are being manipulated to pursue the desires and designs of others. What attracts people to seek power? Sometimes it is the secrecy that enshrouds the manipulation and control of others in work organizations. Other individuals like power because it affords them the opportunity to secure obedience from their subordinates, to command the service or

173

compliance of others. For some, the work situation is the only place where they can acquire and exercise power.

Power struggles and power bases are created within the work setting whenever individuals or groups compete to control the behavior of others. And whenever individuals or groups interact and compete in a power contest, politics are created. Sides are drawn up, parties are developed, people align themselves into formal groups, alliances and coalitions are formed, and the stage is set for a showdown, in which one individual or group wins and all others lose.

The essential characteristic of power as we know it in business and industry today is the manipulation of individuals and groups toward certain ends. Many feel that power is an all-or-nothing phenomenon, a kind of win-lose social process, but this is a misconception, because managers and work groups vary in the amount of power they possess. Moreover, there is variation in how this power is distributed throughout the organizational hierarchy, and how and where and when it can be applied within legitimate areas. For instance, power must be shared by managers and groups in some situations, but not necessarily in others. As an example, managers and their subordinates must work together to reach organizational goals and objectives, if the organization is to survive. But in an effort to reach these goals, they may engage in bitter conflicts which result in power struggles. At times like this, it becomes necessary for a top executive to intervene as judge, and decree which course of action must be followed. Classic examples of this type of intra-organizational power struggles can be found every day between sales and production groups, line and staff managers, and quality control and production managers, to mention a few.

Conflict in the form of power struggles is inevitable and necessary in our complex industrial society. Intra-organizational conflict can often increase the morale of various groups, help them overcome their apathy, and define and enlighten group values and beliefs. The intensive interaction of power struggles keeps groups from becoming isolated or tangential. Power struggles keep organizations efficient and effective so that common ends can be attained. It is when power struggles stop or cease to exist that organizations become inefficient and rigid.

Conflict through intra-organizational power struggles should be a means to an end, and not an end in itself. Whenever power struggles become an end in themselves, dysfunction results. Managers must realize that power struggles should be kept within well-defined limits if they are to be efficient and not detrimental to the overall good of the organization.

Background of power and politics

It is interesting to examine the backgrounds and the patterns of upward mobility various managers and executives have demonstrated and experienced. In many cases, but not all, the home life or the primary group relationships of these people, long before they entered high school, had a great bearing on their quest for power. To be born and raised in a family where one's father was an executive, or a professional manager, compared to a home situation where the breadwinner was a laborer, automatically created a vast differential of social values for the young, ambitious future manager. This is more often the rule than the exception.

Perhaps the most successful power seekers in management today are those who learned the rules and how to play the game early in life. By the time they enter high school, they have developed a consciousness of their social and political self and begin to experiment in the basic arenas of power relationships and politics. High school roles such as homeroom president, editor of the yearbook, captain of an athletic team, or other official positions requiring competition soon teach these youngsters the fundamentals of social power, politics, and responsibility, and in a sense serve as a primary model for their future aspirations and ambitions in business and industry.

How to acquire power through political techniques

There are countless political techniques to gain power in our contemporary industrial organizations. I use the word "political" here to characterize one who is sagacious or shrewd in promoting himself or herself up the organizational hierarchy in order to gain power. Politics are often perceived as an art or science in which shrewdly tactful, cunning, artful, and sometimes dishonest practices must be used in competition against other individuals vying for power and leadership in work group life.

The recent college graduate or management trainee in organizational work institutions must learn to develop connections, coalitions, and alliances with his or her superiors, peer group members, and subordinates. Those who have held early leadership roles can hone their political techniques even finer by carefully studying the following stratagems.

DEVELOPING CONNECTIONS WITH YOUR SUPERIORS

Superiors are the key people to concentrate on. Nobody else in the organization can do more for you than your superior. But how does one go about developing connections with superiors? There are several ways, but the most basic approach is to study the individual whom you wish to make the connection with. Learn as much as you can about his or her background, values, prejudices, hobbies, religion, family, and college attended. More important, you must be able to assess your superior's expectations from his or her subordinates—including you. There is nothing that succeeds better than hard productive work to gain the attention of your superior.

Learning as much as you can about your superior takes time and plenty of effort. But by acquiring bits and pieces of information from here and there, the skillful and shrewd individual soon develops a pattern of past and present behavior upon which to build future plans for getting closer to the boss. During this learning period make mental notes, and if necessary, record the important features at home so they can be studied and reviewed over a period of time. Don't rely on your memory alone. Remember that the boss is a human being, subject to the same emotions, feelings, temperament, frustrations, and anxieties that you are. How the boss reacts is what you want to know, understand, and be able to use for your benefit in the future.

MAKING YOUR HOMEWORK PAY OFF

After carefully studying your superior and learning his or her biases, prejudices, and values, the shrewd subordinate manager or supervisor is careful *never* to offend him or her. This could be a tough and difficult assignment when trying to win your superior's favor and support, because all of us have our own principles, beliefs, and prejudices, but they must never clash with those of your superior.

As you draw closer toward your superior's confidence and feelings, you will find that the boss will try to determine, in very subtle ways, your values and judgments on every controversial issue imaginable. National and international issues concerning religion, economic policies, politics, or racial conflicts are favorite subjects superiors like to discuss with subordinates to determine correlations of thoughts. If you stand on principle and voice your opinions on such testy issues when these opinions are counter to those of your superior, you may find yourself on the periphery of the superior's inner circle.

These seemingly minor encounters are a good test of your past observations and study, and the homework you did on your superior's likes and dislikes. If you've done a good job, you won't be trapped into losing immediate favor with your superior. But if you're caught short on a controversial issue that is not related to your work or the organization, or if you don't want to reveal your opposition, you can fake your way by pleading ignorance of the subject. At times your superior may choose to carry the issue further, and you had better come up with an answer that satisfies him.

USING PEER GROUP MANAGERS

The shrewd manager-politician must learn to build partnerships with other managers in other departments at his or her own level. Primarily the purpose for doing so is to create a web of intelligence gathering as well as a means of support. By tapping these sources daily or weekly, you can gather information affecting various segments of the organization and thus acquire a well-rounded running account of executive thinking and actions. With this intelligence you can anticipate future decisions and probable movements in relation to your own department.

Depending upon who you are, and what part of the organization you function in, it may be possible to help a peer group manager who is in trouble without exerting yourself, or without revealing your true motives. In this manner you build "political mortgages" which can be neatly tucked away in your political bank and recalled, with compounded interest, when you make your move, or gain a higher position within the organization. By the same token, you may allow yourself to be used, within certain limits, by another peer group manager who is politically ambitious but whose direction and final office will not interfere with the office you seek. For instance, a personnel manager may allow himself or herself to be used by an up-and-coming sales manager to get rid of a marginal salesperson, and thus may add another political mortgage to his or her own political bank. By doing someone else's dirty work, the shrewd manager-politician has created an obligation, which should never be forgotten and which can be used at the right psychological moment.

When dealing with peer group managers at your own level and within your own department, the political game requires extremely delicate strategies. Obviously, such factors as age, length of service in the department or on the job, number of subordinates managed, degree of responsibility, degree and type of contribution your group makes to the department, interpersonal relationships with the department head, number of available openings above your position, personalities, and many more, have a bearing on when, where, and how you should make your next move. You must also consider time and timing, which unfortunately are too often overlooked. Many ambitious, impatient individuals tend to show their desires and designs too early in the game, thus allowing the more patient political pro to subtly place many frustrating obstacles in their path.

While marking time, politically ambitious managers should diplomatically build alliances with their own peer group members. Never reveal your plans to other peer group members, and always avoid discussions which directly or indirectly concern upward movement. Analyze your competition keenly, by observing, listening, and making mental notes of their successes as well as their failures. You will always find people among your peers who don't want to engage in this bloody game, thus you eliminate them as competitors, but you can use them as means of support and intelligence gathering.

Above all else, obey the commands and desires of your superiors, and never try to do unusual or "brilliant" things on your own without first obtaining your superior's approval. Second, always make your superior look good, whether he or she is good or not. If your superior is faltering and/or failing there's little to be gained by burying your dagger into his or her back. It is not usually the administrator of the "kiss of death" who succeeds the one he or she politically murdered, but the manager who has built alliances and demonstrated trust and loyalty to his peers, as well as to the now defunct superior. Seldom if ever do the Judas Iscariots win favor and promotion, because they have betrayed not only their superior, but themselves as well.

USING SUBORDINATES

A manager's subordinates, properly used, can be the springboard for upward mobility for the politically ambitious manager. Many of the techniques already mentioned in earlier chapters are means for gaining loyalty, trust, and outstanding work performance. The ability to manage subordinates so as to consistently turn out quality work requires such "political" effort and in a sense is the mark of a true politician—and of a true manager. Managers who can blend the good with the bad, who are willing to negotiate and compromise, who can tolerate the intolerable, who have demonstrated the ability to bring out the best in each individual, and who produce no matter what the odds—these are the types of people top management is always searching for. When managers can accomplish the above on one level, the chances are they can accomplish the same at a higher level within the organization. Loyal and trusting subordinates support their manager not only in the production of work, but also by providing a continual source of internal intelligence through more and better upward communications with their managers. This continual fresh, current, and timely information is essential to the politically ambitious manager if he or she is to succeed and enjoy the fruits of upward mobility and increased power.

Successful political techniques

The following successful political techniques are but a few in a long list that managers must learn to use continuously throughout their careers.

KNOW YOUR JOB AND DO IT WELL

In American business and industry there's probably no better political technique to use than this very simple and basic rule, especially if you expect to survive in the corporate or company political jungle.

One of the biggest problems in management today is that there's too much hot air and not enough follow-through. Many managers substitute empty verbiage for informed action to solve problems, increase production, reduce costs, and train and develop employees into a viable work force. It doesn't work, it has never worked, and it never will work. Today, employees are too intelligent, and too socially aware, and resent being verbally manipulated by their managers about their jobs and work in general. Therefore it behooves you to know your job, what is expected of you, and to produce results. To do this, you must keep your personal radar operating at all times in order to pick up those vital feedback clues and cues that are necessary to function at an optimum rate.

GAIN YOUR SUBORDINATES' LOYALTY

Too many managers assume that each and every subordinate who reports to them is loyal and true blue. This is not necessarily the case. When a subordinate makes an honest mistake, that's one thing, but when a subordinate continually undermines your efforts by "bad-mouthing" you behind your back, or by purposely giving out inadequate information, that's something else. Whenever you step into a higher position, it is imperative that you meet with your subordinates and ask for their loyalty, support, and cooperation. Never assume that subordinates will automatically give you their support and loyalty—to do so is foolhardy. When a newly promoted manager openly asks for support and cooperation, subordinates have little choice but to comply. Those subordinates who choose other alternatives do so at the expense of losing their jobs.

CHOOSE AND DEVELOP YOUR ASSISTANT CAREFULLY

If the job develops to a point that you must choose an assistant, there are many human behavior variables to consider. For the immediate present and short-term future, it is imperative that various technical skills and job knowledge be required. For long-range planning which incorporates your advancement to another position, a manager must consider the training and development of a replacement. Therefore, the assistant you choose must be aggressive enough to want to advance, but loyal and patient enough to spend sufficient time in learning the fundamentals of your position. When you choose assistants, they should be told early in your association with them whether or not they can or cannot advance into your position. This strategy should apply to all levels of management from assistant foremen and supervisors to assistant vice presidents. It should be pointed out to the assistant that loyalty to you must always be the first priority.

If the situation is one in which you are the "transplanted" new manager in new and different surroundings and an assistant has been functioning in the previous manager's role for some time, the techniques required are totally different. In this case, assistants are more concerned about their own security than is the new manager. Many a good assistant has been erroneously swept out the door by the changing of the palace guard! When assistants remain, the probability is that they have maintained some degree of value to the organization, or have strong political ties and reciprocal relations with top-level executives. In rare cases, the new manager may keep them on, but eventually let them go, transfer them, or demote them. In other, extreme cases, the burden of responsibility for directing the ship and the frightening struggle for security rest more heavily upon the assistant than upon the new manager.

Good assistants in these situations tend to demonstrate more loyalty than anyone else within the group, because they're in constant contact with the new manager, and are expected to advise and counsel when requested. Politically intelligent and shrewd assistants will be passive and submissive to the new manager's requests and demands, and above all else, dependent rather than independent in their relations with the new manager. Moreover, they must be willing to quickly learn the demands, expectations, and overall style of the new manager, and to withhold giving advice until asked. Many times they must carry out orders even if the order is counterproductive to past and present policies and procedures of the group or organization.

CHANGE POLITICAL STRATEGIES AS NECESSARY

Let's assume that you as a manager have now reached a new and higher-powered position within the hierarchy. Further, let's assume that you're not an outside "transplant" from another organization, but instead have used various and sundry political techniques to reach this new position. The most important goal you must realize now is survival. You'll probably have from six months to one year, at most, to prove your worthiness and value in this new position. One of the first things you must do is to temporarily lay aside the political "tools" and techniques you used to gain this position, and concentrate on a totally different set of power-political techniques if you expect to survive for long. This very simple fact is one which many politically ambitious managers fail to realize.

USE THE PURSE STRINGS TO CONTROL POWER

As you move up the hierarchy there will come a day when you finally have the opportunity to directly control the purse strings. Many managers have fallen by the wayside because of their lack of knowledge concerning this newly vested power. Politicians outside the business world and from both major political parties have stumbled and fallen because they could not overcome their own personal greed. Likewise, countless thousands of managers in business and industry each year lose their jobs because they are greedy. You must learn how to gain and use power by adroitly controlling large sums of money entrusted to you.

Raises, budgets, variances, expenditures, profit and loss statements, and your effectiveness as a manager can easily be measured by the bottom line figures you develop. If you don't understand all the modern jargon that accountants and auditors use, for goodness' sake ask for help. Learning to use budgets and playing around with variances isn't very hard.

Once you master the language of accounting and auditing, you're in a position to exert power where it really counts. By simply giving or taking away financial support to individuals or groups, you can skillfully manipulate subordinates and peer members as well. This can be done by establishing performance goals that individuals and groups have never achieved before. Making tradeoffs between individuals for more and better performance and giving financial rewards to those who succeed are clean-cut uses of managerial power that are directly tied to control of the purse strings. Know and use such power wisely and with discretion. Salary ranges are created for one thing only, namely, as a tool for managers to practice the "carrot-and-stick" philosophy of organizational power.

Finally, it is necessary at times to be ruthless in the name of managerial expedience, especially where money is involved. By threatening to take away financial support of a group or an individual, or actually taking it away, managers can exercise devastating power and, at least for a short period of time, control subordinate behavior. A short period of time in this sense can be defined as a month to six months. To extend this time period too long may cost you more than you bargained for. Thus, you must keep an ear cocked to the subordinates' attitudes and their work behavior. Suddenly you announce that you have succeeded in obtaining additional funds, and if you are skillful, you become the hero rather than the goat. Organizational financial political power is power at its most sublime level.

BE AN ACTOR AND A SALESMAN

If necessary take up acting, or at least participate in a couple of community, civic, or church-sponsored amateur plays in order to learn the basics of playing roles. Managers who are good at acting can hold their audience's attention and manipulate their thinking and communication processes. By mastering some degree of the acting technique, managers can learn their subordinates' wants and needs and determine their values. Once these wants and needs are known, the political manager can confirm, stall, or deny making any concessions. Furthermore, skillful managers can often sell an individual or group on a goal or objective which, in many cases, is totally different from their original desires. If a discussion by opposing entities ends in an impasse, at least you have entertained the rival factions and they haven't necessarily ended the meeting without achieving anything. Let's examine this political technique more closely.

Let's assume an individual or group presents a proposal which is unacceptable to you as the manager. Enter the actor. First, you paraphrase the request, then you tell a story that is related to the request but that happened years ago. With facial expressions and gestures and talking endlessly, you may mesmerize or captivate your audience. You can inject some humor into your part, and soon the issue, at least temporarily, is removed from the discussion. In effect, you're setting the stage in order to reject the proposal. Finally, you come back to the issue and in a show of open-mindedness, tell your audience that you're receptive to their opinions. You may even jot down some notes to demonstrate your sense of fair play. You must make your audience perceive you as being a fair manager. Repeat a humorous line if necessary, but only to keep your opposition off balance.

Next, be willing to compromise on small issues—a few crumbs here and there may satisfy them. At this point, you inject your ideas and keep repeating them, because repetition is the key to successful salesmanship. Since you've compromised once, your opponents will expect you to compromise a second time. But this is where you reverse the procedure by emphasizing your ability and willingness to compromise, and now the sporting thing for them to do is to compromise. While the opposition is thinking this over, you drive home your final sales pitch and seek to close the deal.

Finally, always remember to radiate self-confidence by making it appear that you know what you're doing, and that you're completely in command of the situation. Between the brilliance you display, the acting you perform, the sales pitch presented, and the vested authority you possess, you're bound to be a successful manager—even though you might have to practice these combined techniques for quite a period of time.

Always keep in mind that the successful politician-manager avoids pressure by placing it upon others. Submit to counsel, but not pressure—especially when you don't deserve it. Learn to use stall tactics when necessary. These can take the form of delaying decisions, diverting questions to other areas, or evading an issue by requesting time to investigate the facts. Other tactics might well include direct frontal approaches such as checking or stopping an individual right in his or her tracks, or countering with an equally pressurized problem.

In conclusion, if you intend to survive in this game of management, you must learn to protect your rear at all times by practicing these and many other successful political techniques.

11 SELF-DEVELOPMENT

Becoming a More Mature Manager

Managers must learn how to know themselves before they can become more successful in industry and business. Learning to know one's self is one thing, making proper assessments of one's self is another, and finally, having the ability and knowledge to develop one's self requires techniques which will be presented in this chapter.

In a recent address before a business group in the Pittsburgh area, James L. Hayes, President of the American Management Associations, posed the question, "Are you doing a good job of whatever it is you do? Chances are you think so but really aren't sure. . . ." Do you know how good a job you're doing? Maybe you do, maybe you don't. Have you established job standards by which you can measure your own performance?

Manager, know thyself

Managers must learn how to develop an internalized reciprocal relationship in order to understand themselves more clearly. This internalized reciprocating learning process must be constantly practiced to be effective when dealing with one's subordinates, peers, and superiors.

To develop an internalized reciprocal relationship means to learn to know your self through interacting with others. Knowing how other people act or react to you, favorably or unfavorably, in your everyday job or work situation is necessary in order for you to know yourself better. Employees' work responses, productivity, and acceptance or rejection of their superiors reflect the attitudes and behavior managers demonstrate toward their subordinates.

Reading others' body language, facial expressions, and inflections in oral communications must be studied carefully and over a long period of time by the manager who wants to succeed. As human beings we can learn to know ourselves only from the reflections and images of ourselves that others transmit back to us.

As managers we must constantly deal with other people. These relationships are based on the interchange of messages via bodily movements, oral communications, and overt self-evaluation, formed on the basis of literally hundreds of thousands of past interacting experiences in life. But if we misjudge or misinterpret these experiences, we cannot have a clear self-evaluation. There are thousands of managers who will live a lifetime harboring self-delusions because they have never learned to establish fair and honest self-evaluations, and thus have never been able to develop fair and honest internalized reciprocal relationships.

How does one learn to develop fair and honest internalized reciprocal relationships? Observe a manager you consider to be successful and you will usually find one who listens intently to others to find clues and facts for solutions to problems, studies facial expressions and body language very carefully, and asks penetrating questions that get to the heart of the problem.

These very simple techniques, developed over many years of managerial practice, reflect a successful manager's ability to review a problem against a fair and honest internalized reciprocal relationship that permits sound and well-thought-out decisions. They are not merely aids to managerial success; they also help managers know themselves more fully as human beings.

What makes a good manager?

Several years ago, in a survey I conducted among several groups of white collar employees in a large manufacturing industry, I asked, "Who was the best manager you ever had?" and "Why?" I received several good answers to the second question, which are listed below:

"He treats all of us as individuals and not like check numbers."

"He keeps his cool—never blows his top, even when I've done something wrong."

"Never chews a guy out in front of others. When you make a mistake he calls you into his office and discusses the mistake thoroughly."

"When you have a work problem he always takes time to sit down and discuss it with you, and usually gives you some good answers."

"He's willing to listen to you and doesn't interrupt you when you're trying to explain something."

"You know exactly where you stand at all times."

"He's understanding and somewhat sympathetic."

"He always takes interest in his people. He always wants to know how you're doing and if he can help."

"If you have an idea about a job and you discuss it with him, and it's worthwhile, he'll tell you so. If the idea wouldn't work, he'll tell you why—he just doesn't say no and leave you hanging without an explanation."

"I liked him because he was not easygoing. When he gave you a job and you did it the way he expected, he would praise you. When you didn't do it the way he expected it to be done, he would tell you why, and where you went wrong. I sure learned a lot from him."

"I respected him because he respected me. He treated me like a human being."

"He was always honest with me, no matter how much it hurt. He would always give me equal authority and responsibility to do a job."

"He made you feel important and your job important as well."

"He praised you when you deserved it."

In a sense, many of these answers are personal techniques that successful managers use. I suggest you review these answers, giving

special attention to the verbs, or action words, used by these employees in describing what makes a good manager. As an individual
who is interested in developing himself or herself into a successful
manager, how many of these techniques do you practice with your
subordinates?

All development is self-development

Self-development is an individual matter. No two persons are exactly the same. Moreover, we all change with time, so that our values
today are not the same as they were two, three, or five years ago. Life
would become stagnant and extremely boring were it not for change
and the need to continue to develop in your present position as a
manager.

Do you seek out new challenges on your job, or are you content to
wait for challenges to present themselves to you? Your answer may
well reflect and determine your success or failure as a manager. Simply stated, our contemporary business and industrial world is constantly in a state of flux—a continually churning, changing state of
affairs. Thus, it behooves the successful manager to inject self-
motivation into his or her program of self-development. To fail to
do so will result in your failure as a manager.

I have always felt very comfortable and needed in an organization
that says, "Your limitations are limitless." In other words, your self-
development and growth are dependent upon your own imagination
and creativity. Obviously, there must be some type of parameters or
limits that you cannot go beyond, but to never reach out and discover
what they are indicates a lack of desire to grow and develop to your
fullest potential.

Have you closely examined the growth opportunities that exist in
management as a means of developing yourself? Discussed below are
a few of the paths to growth and self-development that you should
explore within your own organization.

Your own past management experiences. Consider the new problems, challenges, and obstacles you have had to face in the last 12
months. What have you learned from these experiences? They say
you can never teach an old dog new tricks. Well, maybe that's true

for animals, but human beings, and more especially managers, are never too old to stop learning.

Teaching others. If you want to develop yourself more, take on a training assignment in your own organization. I guarantee that you will learn, develop, and grow as a result of this experience. My own past experiences in the area of training and development have taught me more about business and management in general than any other type of work I have participated in. As a trainer or instructor, you learn more from your students than you probably teach. Why? When you're assigned the job of training employees, you're forced to organize, plan, and dig deep for detailed knowledge and information that you would not be likely to gain in any other way. Managers grow and develop as much in learning to teach others as they do in learning what they teach.

Contacts with your superiors. Whenever your superiors discuss mutual organizational problems with you, you should learn, grow, and develop through their sharing of their experiences, knowledge, and information with you. You may not agree with all their decisions and points of discussion, but you have the opportunity of being exposed to the lessons they impart to you.

Conferences, monthly or weekly management meetings, and plain old "bull sessions" are other means whereby successful managers can incorporate other people's ideas into their own scheme of things.

Contacts with your subordinates. Alert managers can often learn specific details about a particular job or work problem by conferring with their employees. If you want to know how to do a particular job that is done by one of your subordinates, simply ask him or her.

Competition. Ambitious and successful managers who want to move up in the organization will always be aware of their competition. Many times competition creates self-motivation which in turn creates self-development and growth among lower levels of management.

HOW TO MEASURE YOUR OWN SELF-DEVELOPMENT

Much of the development of a manager must be self-development. You may think you are growing and developing within your organization, but not until you have some way of measuring this growth will you really know.

Below is a checklist designed to help you measure the amount of growth and self-development you may have experienced in the past 12 months. Read each question and answer it honestly, checking off one answer. A rating scale follows the checklist to help you evaluate your recent rate of growth.

	Yes	Sometimes	No
1. Have I experienced some degree of growth and self-development in the past 12 months as a result of my present management assignment?	—	—	—
2. Have I tried to improve myself by reading books that are associated with my area of work?	—	—	—
3. Have I tried to improve myself by reading periodicals and journals that are related to my area of work?	—	—	—
4. Have I disciplined myself to the point where I can reason through the majority of my work problems, rather than rely on deep-seated opinions to solve my problems?	—	—	—
5. Have I attempted to improve myself by training or teaching my subordinates?	—	—	—
6. Am I willing to make decisions based on what is best for the organization, rather than who is right?	—	—	—
7. Have I tried to improve both my oral and written communication skills in the past 12 months?	—	—	—
8. Have I developed myself to the point where I can stop feeling frustrated about work problems for which there are no immediate solutions?	—	—	—

9. When interacting with my superiors have I made an attempt to learn some-

	Yes	Sometimes	No
thing new or different about my role in management?	—	—	—
10. When interacting with my subordinates have I tried to learn some specific aspects of their job?	—	—	—
11. Have I taken the opportunity to participate in company-sponsored training programs or outside seminars during the past 12 months?	—	—	—
12. Have I motivated myself to seek ways or methods of growth and self-development?	—	—	—
13. Do I know more than I did 12 months ago about the authority, responsibility, and various duties of my present position?	—	—	—
14. Do I know the parameters of self-development and growth that exist within my organization?	—	—	—
15. Do I have the ability to appraise myself honestly in terms of self-development and growth, and if not satisfied with the results, take steps to correct it?	—	—	—

How to measure and evaluate your score. Give yourself 5 points for every Yes answer; 3 points for every Sometimes answer; and 1 point for every No answer. Grade yourself according to this rating scale:

Your Score	*Interpretation*
70–75	You're doing an excellent job and are probably a successful manager.
60–69	You're above average. Reread the questions and start practicing more self-development and growth in those areas in which you scored low.
40–59	There's still time to make progress.
Below 39	My friend, you need help.

Selected skills for managerial self-development

LEARN HOW TO REMEMBER

Forgetting, or failure to remember names, events, or important dates and data can be very embarrassing to any manager. Managers who openly confess to poor memories really have not learned the material in the first place. Therefore, the very first technique that you must be concerned about when trying to improve your memory is learning how to remember. This requires concentration, the elimination of distractions, self-motivation, repetition, and selecting the important information to be remembered.

For instance, when superiors give you instructions about a new job assignment, listen very carefully, concentrate on their body language, face and eyes, and try to envision the ramifications of the assignment they are describing. Take special note of items you want to remember, such as names, dates, numbers, appointments, and assignments. Practice observing specific details of situations, reports, memos, people, and those things that are important to your total performance. Repeating information back to yourself will help you retain this knowledge through reinforcement.

A desire to remember will obviously help you remember a name, face, event, or important part of your business activity. Motivation also reinforces the internal effort and mental energy needed to insure future recall.

Finally, limit those items you want to learn to remember. By picking and choosing those items you really need, you'll find you will be more capable of remembering what is important to you.

PRACTICE THE GOLDEN RULE

When I am asked to sum up in one sentence what it takes to make a successful manager, my answer is simply, "Practice the golden rule, that is, do unto others as you would have them do unto you." Unfortunately, too many managers distort this rule into "Do unto others *before* they do it to you!" But those who step on people in their mad dash to the top are often kicked out of an organization when the truth about their managerial conduct is known.

Treat your employees the same way you want and expect your superiors to treat you. Individuals at any level are hired because of the skills they bring to the job. All want to be treated with respect. Managers and subordinates alike desire fair and equitable treatment on the job, recognition, praise, patience, and most especially forbearance.

GAIN THE RESPECT OF YOUR EMPLOYEES

The days of the "bull-of-the-woods" managerial philosophy are long gone—thank goodness. This was simply management by fear, not management by respect. As a manager, you cannot make or order your employees to respect you. Respect must be earned by a manager if it is to be genuine and lasting. When you let your subordinates know that you do not have all the answers and you are sincerely willing to listen to their ideas or suggestions, you're on your way to gaining respect. You can also gain respect through exercising tact and diplomacy, sticking up for your subordinates, training, taking a personal interest in your employees, and effective listening. These are not easy tasks—it is much easier to lose subordinates' respect than it is to gain it.

LEARN TO CONTROL YOUR TEMPER AND EMOTIONS

Short-fused managers soon gain a bad reputation and lose respect, breaking down the various successful techniques discussed in this book. Subordinates become fearful, the communication process is totally disrupted, and work becomes drudgery, rather than fun. Managers who constantly have temper tantrums or display wild irrational behavior are either sick (physically or mentally) or totally incompetent. In time, the experienced, long-term subordinate soon learns how to "play the boss," and develops successful techniques to circumvent these forms of immature, childish behavior. In effect, it is the subordinate who manages the business at hand, not the manager. Managers who continually lose their tempers, however, are likely to find themselves looking for new employment in another organization.

LEARN TO FORGIVE AND FORGET

Successful managers make mistakes. In fact, they make mistakes every day, but they also learn from these errors of commission or omission. That's why they are successful. Likewise, subordinates make mistakes, but it is the manager's task to train errant employees, not to continually remind them of their errors.

Very few "wrong" decisions that resulted in poor performance by any number of subordinates have ever caused an organization to go into bankrupcy. (Organizations fail because top management makes too many "wrong" decisions.) But I have seen many managers bankrupt a subordinate's pride and feeling of self-esteem because they would not forgive and forget some petty, ridiculous mistake that was made by the subordinate.

Equalization in the treatment of employees by forgiving and forgetting is an important technique that successful managers must learn and practice daily. Obviously, the individual who, after proper training, continues to make the same error repeatedly must be reprimanded, removed, or placed on a different job. Successful managers get to know their employees, practice patience through training, and are able to assess an individual's performance in a relatively short period of time. Thus they are capable of making good decisions about an individual that will be beneficial to the employee, the work group or organization, and the manager.

LEARN TO OBSERVE ACCURATELY

Too many managers believe wholeheartedly in the old proverb, "Seeing is believing." But in today's business world, seeing can be deceiving. As managers, and more particularly human beings, we often see what we want to see, or we see what we expect to see. Sometimes, in trying to understand the components of a problem, we fail to comprehend the overall problem—we can't see the forest for the trees.

Learning to be more accurate in what you observe is a self-development technique that must be practiced constantly. Too often we "look at" a problem, or "watch" an operation, and make decisions to act on the basis of such quasi observations, only to be proved wrong. We observe life with all our senses, personal feelings, and past experiences, which inevitably cloud our objectivity. Moreover, we all have certain fears, likes and dislikes, and personal desires, which differ from those of our superiors, peers, and subordinates. Thus, when decisions must be made, especially concerning the interactions of employees, successful managers take into account their emotions and limitations, as well as the limitations of others. Here are two techniques that will help you become a more accurate observer:

1. Set aside a certain amount of time each day and force yourself to carefully and thoroughly examine the structure and functions of the work you manage. Break down the general work items into specific job elements. If need be, write the main job elements down on a piece of paper. Next, mentally place the questions of "What?" "Why?" "Where?" "When?" "Who?" and "How?" in front of each job element. If you can answer these questions logically and with a high degree of accuracy, you're a good observer. When you find you have difficulty in answering part or all of one of these questions, it's generally an indication you've failed to observe accurately.

2. Concentrate on identifying those items that are most important to you in the work you manage. For instance, if you're at a job site, or reviewing a report, ask yourself, "What are the important items I should look for?" Now close your eyes for a few seconds and try to "see," through the use of mental images, those same items of importance. "Burn" those items into your brain by heavy and deep concentration. Repeat the process several times (at home, too) until you can mentally recall the items with complete accuracy. You must work at this technique continually if you want to be successful at it.

Finally, for reinforcement purposes, you must take action and make decisions based on those items you have learned to accurately observe. By combining the two techniques described above (self-questioning and concentration) with decision-making, you'll form the habit of looking at things and analyzing what needs to be done.

LEARN TO BE FLEXIBLE

Do you use rigid habits of doing your job as a manager? Or do you use creative solutions and perhaps different ways of attacking problems? Is the need for an orderly system keeping you from carrying out your responsibilities? Perhaps you're not flexible enough in the way you approach your job, or perhaps you're too flexible.

MEASURING YOUR MANAGERIAL FLEXIBILITY

Listed below are several questions designed to measure your degree
of managerial flexibility. Check either a Yes or a No answer for each
question. A self-evaluation scale on your degree of flexibility follows
this questionnaire.

	Yes	No
1. I occasionally vary the route when I drive home from work.	—	—
2. I enjoy working with people who have very definite ideas about how the work should be done.	—	—
3. Once I begin a job or project, I hate to change the way I am doing it.	—	—
4. I try to be meticulous in everything I do.	—	—
5. I like to see my subordinates plan and organize new assignments I give them.	—	—
6. Once I start on a project at work, I have no difficulty staying with it.	—	—
7. I always search for the one best method to solve my problems at work.	—	—
8. I think that organizational policy and procedures should be adhered to as much as possible.	—	—
9. Once a work rule is made, you should stick with it.	—	—
10. I know exactly what I'll be doing five years from now.	—	—
11. I like to know exactly what I am going to do at the start of every work day, but I am also capable of making adjustments during the day.	—	—
12. I think that tardiness is a characteristic of a lackadaisical person.	—	—
13. I always have my reports, monthly statements, and work assignments done on time.	—	—
14. I think that new ideas are O.K., but it takes a lot of additional work to execute them and usually the results are the same.	—	—

	Yes	No

15. I am always looking for new ideas and new ways to do things both at home and at work. ___ ___

16. I think that successful managers work smarter, not harder. ___ ___

17. I think that successful managers do things the way they've been done in the past. ___ ___

18. Sometimes I like to go to work early so that I can get a jump on things. ___ ___

19. I find it frustrating at times when my superiors do not accept new and different ways of doing things. ___ ___

20. I think at the end of a day your desk should be cleaned off and everything put away. ___ ___

21. I think that labor contracts and safety rules were written for a specific reason and must be adhered to at all times. ___ ___

Evaluation. If you answered Yes less than five times you may be too flexible. If you answered No less than five times you may be too rigid in the performance of your job. Successful managers need a wholesome mixture of both order and flexibility in their style.

A manager's style is simply defined as the modus operandi, or the mode of operating or working, that a manager chooses to develop. Make no mistake about it, your style affects the behavior of your subordinates. Hard-driving, tough-minded managers who create fear among their subordinates can expect corresponding reactions in return, whereas overpermissive managers become totally engrossed in people problems to the exclusion of production goals. Strange as it may seem, such a permissive managerial style is not always valued too highly by the majority of one's subordinates. In fact, there may be the tendency by subordinates to take undue advantage of this style of managing. Therefore, what's a good style to develop?

In our contemporary work world, the manager who gives equal concern to both performance goals and people problems will be successful. This modus operandi permits managers a very high degree of flexibility over a longer period of time. The fact that our world is constantly changing as a result of the ebb and flow of worldwide economics and inflation causes changes in corporate objectives, which filter downward and in turn result in alterations to managers' plans and goals. Therefore, today's managers must be willing to develop and practice change and flexibility in their styles.

12 TIME MANAGEMENT

Dealing with Our Most Irreplaceable Natural Resource

Benjamin Franklin is credited with making the following statement concerning time, "Dost thou love life? If so, do not squander time, for that's the stuff life's made of." Others have defined time as that systematic relationship in which one event relates to another event and is expressed as past, present, or future. All of us every day hear such expressions as "Don't waste time," "What time is it?" "Time is money, and money is time," "Watch your time," "You're late!" or "You're early!" "Spend your time wisely," "Putting in time," and so forth.

Regardless of how people talk about time, the fact remains that we all have exactly the same amount of time in an eight-hour day. The major problem facing all managers is not the acknowledgment of this time factor, but what managers do with the time they have—in other words, how well managers utilize this most irreplaceable natural resource.

The uniqueness of this valuable resource is frightening, because we cannot accumulate time like money. We are forced to utilize it, whether we want to or not, because we cannot turn it off and on like water from a faucet. Time is irrevocable, irretrievable, and unrepealable. Furthermore, when we fail to use it properly, we end up losing it entirely—because time waits for no one. Thus we will treat time as a resource in this chapter and concentrate on "time-proven" successful techniques.

The ominous pitfalls of time management

Work, and the management of work, must in the last true sense be creative. It cannot always be patterned or simply reduced to a routine. Our contemporary work world will not permit it. Work that is too routine is soon computerized, and the jobs of the people who originally did it are eliminated. Furthermore, new opportunities for management creativity are constantly challenging professional and executive managers. In fact, many managers are actually doing some degree of creative work without realizing it.

Managers are paid to collect facts, review reports, use their judgment, and make decisions when solving problems that affect the organization. Thus, the creative work required by managers cannot be produced or even measured by the hour or the day, in the way that work by blue collar employees can. For example, professional personnel managers and those engaged in training and development endeavors are faced with unstructured time frames or parameters, and are often apprehensive that they cannot justify their existence on the payroll, much less prove the contributions they make to the organization. Yet, the organizational requirement of "recording time worked," or "putting in time," can lead to ominous pitfalls in one's managerial philosophy. Some of them are discussed here.

ACTIVITY VS. PRODUCTIVE WORK

Creative managers, and that's what most managers are today, are paid good salaries for "putting in time." Obviously, these managers will find something to do with their time, but the end product of their efforts may be totally useless or unacceptable to the organization's goals. Thus, time-consuming activity by a group of managers or a single manager does not always result in productive work. Meetings are often excellent examples of fruitless, time-consuming activity.

It is truly frustrating to consider the meetings, reports, surveys, fact-finding investigations, and other activities that are preordained or invented by thousands of managers in the name of work. Although this activity keeps several subordinates extremely busy, organizations collect more facts and figures than they can ever hope to use. Unfortunately, very few managers take sufficient time to think through a problem and request that only pertinent information be collected and analyzed. Thus, hundreds of hours of diligent work are squandered in the final analysis.

THE TYRANNY OF TIME

Time becomes tyrannical when weak and incompetent managers allow it to rule their lives, their leadership styles, and their effectiveness, whereas strong and competent managers master time by exercising their power to plan and budget their time. Those who permit time to master their lives are often given to distorted judgments and snap decisions concerning organizational problems. As a result of poor or ineffective planning of their time, incompetent managers must continually struggle to meet deadlines, and are constantly putting out small brush fires while putting in their required time on the job. Such comments as, "I never seem to have enough time to get things done," or "Time will not permit me to finish that assignment" are made by managers who accept time as their master, not by managers who have learned to master the tyranny of time and make it work for them.

TIME AS A DEMORALIZING FACTOR

Managers who continually fail to utilize their time properly find their efforts frustrating and demoralizing. When no attempt is made to change this pattern of behavior it soon becomes a vicious circle. Managers put in more time and accomplish less, and begin to lose their perspective. They are reduced to a state of weakness, disorganization, and a loss of self-discipline, resulting in still less productive and meaningful work. In extreme situations, managers may develop into "workaholics," or suffer irreparable physical and mental impairment to themselves.

Time can also be a demoralizing factor to older managers who realize that they have not achieved the goals and objectives once sought. Provided sufficient longevity, all managers must one day lay aside their tools of labor and years of experience and make room for others to succeed them. To many managers this is most difficult, although they will not admit it. Instead, they boast about looking forward to retirement and the "good life," but inwardly they have difficulty coming to terms with the approaching "autumn season" of their lives.

One costly and totally devastating mistake that contemporary management makes is the failure to capitalize on the years of experience accumulated by older managers. Many organizations fail to properly prepare junior executives to replace their older seniors who retire. In many cases this preparation through formalized training and development could take years to accomplish. Instead, organizations bring in "outsiders" with so-called fresh and new ideas but only after the real "pro" has retired. Injection of new but inexperienced blood may or may not succeed, but, if it fails, additional time and money have been wasted, palace revolts occur, and turnover of the cadre suddenly increases, not to mention the disruption and disorganization that develop.

Techniques that avoid the pitfalls

Assume a more relaxed posture about the concept of time. Instead of trying to force creative work into time parameters, organizations might be wise to assume a more relaxed posture toward the time spent and concentrate on the results achieved. Creative management cannot be produced on demand or within prescribed time frames. When managers are required to show results for their time spent on creative problem solving, a very dangerous muddling of means and ends results. If, during creative management exercises, especially in the infant stages of a project, the results seem intangible, human behavior dictates that more concrete evidence be produced, and thus time itself can become a false symbol of the anticipated results. "How soon can you install that system?" or "We've got to get it done by the end of the month"—these are common expressions of time pressures which tend to confuse not only the process for obtaining the results, but also the results as well.

Learn to think through various jobs to determine the time required. Managers must learn to think through the various jobs they are to work on, so as to anticipate the time it will take to complete the job. Some work requires a fixed time schedule, while other work does not. A completely new job, never before attempted, and/or one that requires creativity based on trial and error or lack of experience are examples of the latter type of planning. Whether a job has a fixed time schedule or not, a successful manager will make the difference clearly known to his superiors, peers, and subordinates. This must be the first step in thinking through various jobs to be completed. Once a determination is made, the decision(s) must then be communicated to those employees who will perform the work.

Develop double deadlines to get the work out on time. After projected time schedules have been determined for jobs with either a fixed time schedule (normally the quasi-routine) or a nonfixed time schedule (the new job requiring creativity), successful managers should develop the double deadline technique, arbitrarily selecting a primary due date and a final due date. The primary due date, which is simply a warning device that managers keep to themselves, may be marked on a calendar or desk pad, and as the date or designated time approaches, the manager surveys what has been accomplished up to that point in time.

The primary due date can serve many purposes, such as determining revisions on the final due date, adjusting work schedules, or anticipating quicker completion dates. This may also entail placing the project on a higher priority basis, and then subdividing the project into specific phases, each of which is again assigned primary due dates and final due dates.

Use tickler files that tackle first and tickle second. Most successful managers who deal with outside organizations or a multiplicity of projects use some type of a tickler filing system to ensure timely follow-up. The best and simplest tickler file consists of 31 folders, one for each day of the month. Reminders of everything to be handled on a specific date are placed in the appropriately dated folder. This includes reminders of both business and personal or family affairs.

Managers who use a tickler system realize that they must tackle first, at the start of each day, each reminder, then tickle second all future reminders. The establishment of a tickler system is quite easy, but the self-discipline required to maintain and utilize it properly is what distinguishes the successful from the not-so-successful manager.

Techniques for saving time

You probably know or have met someone who has the reputation of getting things done. A close observation or a frank discussion with this individual would probably reveal that he or she understands the value of time, knows how to use it, and receives a great deal of self-satisfaction from accomplishing so much in relatively short periods of time. Closer observation and/or discussion would probably reveal that this individual realizes the value of planning, organizing, and self-motivation, but most important of all has learned to use time-saving techniques such as the ones described below.

Short memos. Learn to say more with fewer words, especially when constructing a memo. Effective memos should be about one paragraph long. Approximately four or five sentences should get the message across. Whenever possible, answer a memo by writing a short reply on the original memo you received, then make a copy of the memo and get it on its way. This is faster than writing a second memo in response to the first memo.

Phone, rather than walk, drive, or write. Because we all live in an advanced technological world we should use the modern miracles of communication to save time and money. Over the years, I've known several managers who travel to other plant locations and branch offices to check out certain projects, when they could have telephoned to get the necessary information. While it is true that a face-to-face conversation is the best method of communicating, the telephone, telegram, or TWX message can be a substitute for many time-consuming visitations.

Organize your telephone call before you make it. It's important that you organize a telephone call before making it, especially if it's long distance. Simply note certain key words that represent important items to discuss with the individual you're calling. As these items are discussed, simply check them off or cross them out until the discussion is concluded. It's very frustrating, costly, and extremely time-consuming to have to call the other person back because you forgot to ask an important question.

Learn to shuffle papers correctly. Every time you pick up, read, or put down a piece of paper without doing anything constructive about it is a waste of time. Some successful managers I've known separate their mail, memos, and paperwork into three action piles, classified into the following categories: (1) take immediate action because it is necessary; (2) hold for future action, perhaps tomorrow or next week because it is not a high priority; and (3) discard the junk mail or trivial paperwork into a wastepaper basket.

Learn to utilize your commuting time. If you use public transportation such as a bus or train, you probably have a couple of hours each week to utilize as you go to and from work. The success of this technique depends on your ability to form the habit of utilizing this time frame, rather than wasting it.

If you drive to work, there are a couple of techniques you might consider. First, read while you drive! Sounds kind of impossible, but consider the minutes you lose at red lights, or in backed-up traffic at busy intersections. I know a gentleman who told me he could scan *The Wall Street Journal* in five to eight minutes by reading the important sections while waiting at busy intersections or at red lights. Today, he's chairman of the board of a very large and diversified corporation. Another technique is to prerecord important and succinct messages on a cassette tape recorder at home, and play these back while driving to work. As one manager put it, "It's better than listening to all that junk music and advertising on the car radio." Obviously, he didn't do this every day, but only on certain days when he had to visit a client or make a presentation to a special group of individuals.

Use the closed-door policy. You have heard about the "open-door" policy that encourages subordinates to walk into their managers' office and discuss work problems. The "closed-door" policy is used by managers who need privacy and wish to utilize their time undisturbed. When very important study, reading, or decision making is required, and only you are equipped to do it, it makes sense to close the door. By making yourself inaccessible, and in a sense turning your back on your subordinates, you very clearly indicate the need to be alone so that you can maximize time to its fullest.

Pick the appropriate time to schedule meetings. When you schedule a meeting late in the afternoon, perhaps an hour before quitting time, most of your subordinates are champing at the bit to get home. Thus, what may have taken two or three hours in the morning to cover in the meeting, may only take an hour or less to cover late in the afternoon. Managers must decide the relative importance of the meeting, its agenda, and its effects.

For example, if the purpose of the meeting is to discuss a new labor contract agreement of great importance, with changes that will cover a period of three years, then it would be proper to schedule a more lengthy meeting in the morning. If, on the other hand, the meeting is called to announce a modification of a policy or procedure, which is of lesser importance than a new labor contract, call it later in the afternoon.

Delegate work to save your time. One of the greatest time savers is getting someone else to do the work for you. Since I covered this subject of delegation in Chapter 5, I will not belabor the point here. However, managers should consider delegating those areas of work they themselves have done in the past and which are routine. Effective delegation requires proper training and coaching if the work is to be done correctly.

Always be aware of and respect the time alloted to the subordinate to whom you delegate part of your responsibility. In many cases, the major portion of a subordinate's work schedule has been preplanned by the manager in advance. By adding additional work projects one can interrupt a priority work schedule and cause a loss of time perspective. Again, what may appear to be simple and routine for you, because of your experience, may well be viewed as a major project by a less experienced subordinate who is trying to prove his or her worth.

Learn to estimate time. As a former industrial engineer for a large steel-producing company, I soon learned how to measure time requirements on certain jobs. After several time studies it became quite easy to realistically estimate how long certain jobs would take. Perhaps the most surprising thing I learned after two or three years was the fact that most work requirements take about 50 percent of an eight-hour day. Other work-related activities such as attention time, stand-by time, and rest and personal allowance time were not considered productive, but consumed the other 50 percent of an eight-hour work day.

Most of us tend to underestimate the time involved for a work project we like to do and to overestimate the time involved for work projects that we don't like to do. In many cases it becomes a matter of self-deception and we would be better off to tackle the jobs we don't like first, and save the ones we like best to do last. In a sense, this would be a means of rewarding ourselves, because once accomplished, the work we think we dislike is self-rewarding when we know it's out of the way. Thus we can enjoy a higher degree of job satisfaction.

Define work goals. Psychologists tell us, as a result of experiments, that when work goals are poorly defined or vague, time on a job moves slower than when the work goals are clear and well defined. Thus, managers should clearly define work goals for their subordinates. This technique will actually make work appear to be shorter because subordinates have a yardstick or standard against which they can measure their progress. Furthermore, motivation becomes stronger as subordinates get closer to achieving the work goal.

Keeping one's subordinates busy, however, does not always result in progress. Successful managers always relate to their subordinates how their work performance fits into the department, and the relation of the department to the whole organization. When subordinates underestimate the importance of their jobs, managers should clarify these factors and redefine their work goals. Comment about their progress to date, indicate where the individual or group is heading, and tactfully explain in terms of time how far along the project has advanced.

Managers should be willing to tell and show their subordinates how they can manipulate time to their advantage. Perhaps short-cuts can be made, or minor work projects can be laid aside and coupled up with more advanced steps as the project nears completion. Such interest and information on the part of managers will serve as a stimulus to subordinate supervisors and employees and result in greater individual incentive and job satisfaction.

Analyze the way you utilize your time. There are many reasons why managers don't have enough time, or don't make full use of the time they have. Such time-consuming activities as devoting disproportionate amounts of time to routine tasks, lack of delegation, and poor planning and organization are some of the reasons for mismanaging one's time on the job. One of the biggest reasons, however, is the failure to analyze how you utilize your time. If you know you're constantly behind and you feel that you lack time, try conducting a brief analysis of the way you spend each working day for the next four weeks. It's not necessary to construct time-distribution charts and plot every half hour or fifteen minutes during this self-analysis. Instead, here are a couple of simple questions you should address to yourself at the end of each work day:

1. Did I get everything done today that I had planned?
2. If I didn't get everything done today that I had planned, what were the main reasons?
3. What do I plan to accomplish tomorrow?

With regard to the first two questions, you should make notes on the reasons you failed to accomplish what you had planned for each day. At the end of the four-week period you will find that you have constructed a meaningful pattern of time-wasting activities that interfere with your utilization of time. Where a high frequency of repeated obstacles appears, you then must take corrective action.

This technique will help you identify those areas that are costing you valuable time. However, this technique is dependent upon your willingness to ask yourself those three questions and to keep records or notes each day, so that obstacles and patterns of behavior can be identified. In addition, you could review earlier parts of this chapter and put into practice other techniques discussed, as a means of taking corrective action.

Negative personal traits that waste time

All managers have certain idiosyncrasies and work habits that interfere with the proper use of their time. Successful managers have long recognized these negative personal traits and have put them aside, so that they no longer become obstacles to their careers. A discussion of some of these negative personal traits follows.

Striving for perfection. Trying to be absolutely perfect in your job can cost you endless hours of wasted time. In extreme situations, the perfectionist loses sight of the goals and inadvertently adds more time to a project than is needed.

Excessive self-inflicted tension. We live in a tension-filled world, so why add self-inflicted tensions? Excessive tensions create unneeded physical and mental fatigue that we must constantly combat. They reduce available time for creative and productive work, because they interfere with our thought processes and thus with our ability to accomplish our goals.

Worry, frustration, and even hostility are excellent examples of the types of self-inflicted tensions that one should try to avoid. By directly attacking these problems, one can often solve or modify them.

Making excuses for past failures. Some of the most successful managers I've known have made numerous mistakes and suffered from many past failures, but today they are successful because they learned from their past errors. They didn't waste their time by making excuses or trying to explain away past failures—so why should you?

Indecisiveness. Indecisiveness, or the inability to make decisions, leads directly to procrastination. You waste your own time and hold up those who are waiting for your decision. Make the decision—right or wrong—but for goodness' sake, make it!

Summary

What does it cost you to waste time? As a manager, you're paid to make decisions and solve problems with the least expenditure of time in order to help your organization stay competitive.

Assuming you live long enough to retire and enjoy the fruits of your labor, do you know, or realize, how many hours you have to spend in your work career? For the sake of this discussion let's assume you work for 40 years at a minimum of 2,000 hours per year. That totals 80,000 hours in your career, give or take a few thousand. How many of these 80,000 hours have you spent up to this point? How many of the remaining hours can you afford to waste? What do you want to accomplish in your remaining hours? Once you have thought about these questions, go back and answer my opening question—What does it cost you to waste time?

Since time, in one sense, is an economic resource that unfortunately cannot be expanded or contracted, recovered, or replaced, a great deal of what is termed "cost" in management is the cost of time. Therefore, what does it cost you to waste time?

Your attitude about the past, present, and the future will have more effect upon your accomplishments than any other single factor. Obviously, there's nothing you and I can do about the past—except to learn from our past successes and failures. Thus, lingering on past accomplishments and/or failures at the expense of present and future goals and objectives is a frightful waste of time. The present, the "here and now," is very fleeting. But the future permits managers to manipulate this valuable economic resource, to escape from the irreversibility of the past and the limitations of the present. The future is the arena in which managers have the opportunity to become more successful. Therefore, the greatest contribution managers can make to the organization for which they work, as well as to themselves, is to constantly improve the utilization of their time and the individuals they manage.

HOW YOU MEASURE THE VALUE OF TIME

Below is a lengthy checklist designed to help you measure the value of time and the skill with which you manage your time. Read each question and answer it honestly. At the end of the checklist you will find a guide to evaluate your score.

	Yes	Sometimes	No
1. Do you assign priorities to the various jobs you are expected to do?	___	___	___

	Yes	Sometimes	No
2. Do you delegate routine work that you have done before to your subordinates?	—	—	—
3. Do you utilize part of your time training subordinates?	—	—	—
4. When giving instructions to your subordinates do you tailor the instructions to the individual?	—	—	—
5. Do you usually construct memos that are one paragraph long?	—	—	—
6. Do you try to estimate the time it will take to perform certain jobs?	—	—	—
7. Do you use the double deadline technique to plan and control your work schedules?	—	—	—
8. When you receive a memo that requires an answer, do you answer on the original memo, make a copy of it, and return it to the sender?	—	—	—
9. Do you use the telephone frequently to save time on various work projects?	—	—	—
10. Do you organize your telephone calls, especially on important matters, before making the call?	—	—	—
11. Do you have a systematic technique for handling your mail, memos, and other pieces of paper?	—	—	—
12. Have you formed the habit of utilizing your commuter time to its fullest extent when traveling to and from work?	—	—	—
13. If you drive to work rather than use public transportation, have you developed any techniques that will enable you to better utilize this time?	—	—	—
14. Do you use the closed-door policy as a means of maximizing your time to its fullest?	—	—	—

	Yes	Sometimes	No

15. Do you consider yourself the master of your time?   ___   ___   ___

16. Are your most alert hours at work spent on relatively important tasks?   ___   ___   ___

17. Do you believe that managers' attitudes toward themselves and others will influence how much effort and time they put into getting things done?   ___   ___   ___

18. Do you believe that a great deal of time is wasted by managers who attend unnecessary meetings?   ___   ___   ___

19. Do you believe that managers should make some type of evaluation of the present and future demands on their time?   ___   ___   ___

20. Do you believe that the plea of "lack of time" is an alibi for one who procrastinates?   ___   ___   ___

21. When performing your job do you permit chance circumstances to determine what to do next?   ___   ___   ___

22. Do you believe that budgeting time can be defined as deciding in advance what to do with your available minutes, hours, and days?   ___   ___   ___

23. Do you believe that managers who get a lot of things done know and practice time management?   ___   ___   ___

24. Have you ever analyzed how you spend your time at work?   ___   ___   ___

25. Do you believe that time like money is to be spent judiciously if one is to get the most value in return?   ___   ___   ___

26. Have you ever asked yourself this question at the end of a work day: "Did I

	Yes	Sometimes	No
get everything done today that I had planned?''	___	___	___
27. Have you ever asked yourself this question at the end of a work day: "If I didn't get everything done today that I had planned, what were the basic reasons?''	___	___	___
28. Have you ever insisted that your subordinates complete orders, invoices, or requisitions that are readable, accurate, and complete in an effort to avoid wasting time?	___	___	___
29. Have you ever tried to identify obstacles that interfere with the utilization of your time?	___	___	___
30. Have you ever analyzed the amount of time you spend on routine matters?	___	___	___
31. Have you ever attempted to show your subordinates how they can manipulate their time to their advantage?	___	___	___
32. Do you believe that when a work goal is poorly defined or vague, time appears to be longer?	___	___	___
33. Do you believe that as you approach the completion of a work project, time appears to be shorter for the same rate of progress?	___	___	___
34. Do you believe that clearly defining a work goal tends to make the time spent on the project seem shorter?	___	___	___
35. Do you believe that telling your subordinates what you expect of them will provide them with criteria by which to measure their own results?	___	___	___

36. Do you believe that, as managers, we tend to underestimate the time involved

	Yes	Sometimes	No
for what we like to do and overestimate the time for what we don't like to do?	⎯	⎯	⎯

37. Do you believe that successful managers take the attitude that the more time they save, the more time they will seek to save?   ⎯   ⎯   ⎯

38. Do you believe that the best time-saving technique is to do things immediately and not postpone them?   ⎯   ⎯   ⎯

39. Do you believe that making better use of your time requires changes in your attitudes and work habits?   ⎯   ⎯   ⎯

40. Do you believe that wanting to save time is the secret of successful time management?   ⎯   ⎯   ⎯

Scoring and evaluation. Give yourself 5 points for every Yes answer; 3 points for every Sometimes answer; and 1 point for every No answer. Grade yourself according to this rating scale:

Your Score	*Interpretation*
200–190	You're right on target and are probably a highly successful manager.
189–170	You have a good sense of the value of time management.
169–140	Work on it, my friend—there is still hope.
139 and under	Did you lose your watch, or your awareness of time management?

INDEX